30
WAYS to
IGNITE
YOUR

in 30 DAYS

COPYRIGHT STATEMENT

30 Ways to Ignite Your Legacy © Lady JB Owen- June 2024

Published and printed by Ignite Publishing™
Red Deer, AB
Canada, T4N1S1 www.igniteyou.life

Editor-in-Chief JB Owen
Book and Cover design by Kristine Joy Magno and Siniša Poznanović
Edited by JB Owen, Mimi Safiyah, Zoe Wong, and Steph Elliott
Designed in Canada
ISBN: 979-8-9872121-9-6

Ordering Information: Quantity sales. Special discounts are available on quantity purchases by corporations, associations, and others. For details, contact the publisher at the above address. Programs, products, or services provided by the authors are found by contacting them directly.

GOOGLE is a trademark of **GOOGLE INC.**
APPLE is a trademark of **Apple Inc.**
YOUTUBE is a trademark of **GOOGLE LLC.**
LINKEDIN is a trademark of **LinkedIn Corporation.**

Testimonials

I wish to pay tribute to a remarkable woman who changed the trajectory of my life. Six years ago, we met amongst the bean bags in the auditorium in Tallinn, Estonia. I was shy and awkward. I did not know anyone in the sea of faces of 1000 people from 53 countries. But Lady JB was the first to welcome me with warmth and generosity. She was simply luminous. One year later, we met again in Pula, Croatia, with another 1000 people from 50 different countries. She looked deeply into my eyes and handed me my first copy of a book in which I had written a chapter and she had published; she looked at me and said, "You are a writer."

Those words I will never forget. You see, Lady JB ignited my courage after not having written for thirty years. I had worked as a political journalist in my youth. But somewhere along the line, someone had told me that my writing was "Too melodramatic." And so I diminished my voice. I made myself small, flattened my flamboyance, and became more invisible. I would do anything to fit in and not stand out. But under Lady JB's curation, my writer's voice tentatively scripted words onto the page. I was becoming a writer again.

Years later, I had the opportunity to attend a remarkable Global Speakers Summit in Las Vegas organized by Lady JB. I shared a series of stories I had never spoken of in my home in South Africa. Somehow, I knew this tribe of speakers, this tribe of love, would be a gentle landing for a poignant message—the key moments that had awakened my political activism as a 19-year-old growing up in Apartheid South Africa. I spoke about the power of words and the power of stories to change the world. And in doing so, I changed *my* world.

When I finished speaking, most of the people in the audience were in tears; the Master of Ceremonies was so overcome that she could not speak. I knew God had gifted me this voice and that he had led me there. It was a pivotal moment in my life, the culmination of a dream born six years ago when JB whispered in my soul that maybe I did have a bigger story to tell. It took 30 years to have the courage to tell my story. The book *Belonging* is now my legacy.

You have been pivotal in my story, JB. I honor the remarkable woman you are, knighted for your humanitarian work and an unstoppable force of nature. I thank you for your furnace of faith and your effervescent fun, your kilometers of courage, and above all, for your vision to truly leave a legacy. You have ignited millions of people around the world with stories of hope and healing. You are building schools of empowerment all over the world. But you have changed this one life more than you will ever know.

Alison Weihe

Award-winning Entrepreneur, Speaker, Transformational Leadership Coach, and Author of BELONGING

Lady JB Owen's book, '30 Ways to Ignite Your Legacy in 30 Days,' has been a refreshing read that deeply resonated with me. It's not often you come across a book that not only inspires but also provides practical steps to make a real impact. I found JB Owen's writing style to be clear and engaging, making complex ideas about legacy-building accessible and actionable. What struck me most about this book is its ability to spark new ideas and motivate action. Before reading it, I had not fully considered how I could intentionally create a legacy that aligns with my values and goals.

The book's straightforward approach helped me clarify my thoughts and set meaningful goals for myself. The advice and tips shared throughout the pages are invaluable. They are not just theoretical concepts but practical strategies that can be implemented immediately. Whether it's improving personal skills, nurturing relationships, or contributing positively to the community and world at large, JB Owen's insights have empowered me to take concrete steps forward. This book ' is more than a self-help book; it's a guide that encourages personal growth and inspires a desire to positively impact the world.

Renee Dutton

Two-time International Bestselling Author of "The Sunshine Effect™," Founder, and TV Show Host at The Positivity Report™

JB is a gift to the world. Her commitment to supporting those who dream of making a big difference in the world is unwavering. I am honored to be her friend and supporter in her journey to ignite humanity's consciousness, her desire to do good, and create a better world for everyone. I'd definitely read every word she writes—her mastery is brilliant!"

Dame Doria
(DC) Cordova, PhD (Hon.) and CEO Owner Excellerated Business Schools® / Money & You®

So many people talk about igniting legacy, and now you get the 30 hands-on ways to ignite your legacy *in 30 days* with the expert Lady JB Owen. You will want to listen to what she has to say and read what she has to share as this is someone who is truly making a difference for all of humanity.

Brigitta Hoeferle
CEO Center of Training, Int'l Speaker, Master Certified Coach (MCC)

Lady JB knows the power of purpose before profit, helping others, and putting them first. She comes from a place of a servant's heart. Her honesty, the message of kindness, and the love that she gives resonates with me very much. I know we can change the world one person at a time. If we do this together, there'll be a ripple effect throughout the globe. And I completely feel that JB is a torch bearer. Her kindness, gratitude, and compassion are always there for people. I'm very happy to say she is my friend, and I support her in everything she does to build legacies.

Craig Shah
CEO CS Beverly Hills, Founder ELEVATE™ Mastermind, and Founder EVOKE Immersive Technologies™

Collaborating with Lady JB ct has been an absolute privilege. Her unwavering passion for bringing our collective voices to the forefront by motivating and empowering others was palpable at every step of the journey. I am genuinely grateful for the opportunity to work with such a dedicated individual committed to a profound mission. I extend my heartfelt gratitude to Lady JB for providing this platform that unites us through our stories and kindles the greatness within each of us.

Farrah Smith
Life Coach, and Philanthropist

I was introduced to Lady JB Owen at a time in my life when I was bobbing along life like a piece of driftwood on the ocean tide. Lady JB gently guided me in telling my story; she has a unique gift. She not only has the power of the pen, but she knows how to gift that power to others. She has changed my life, as well as so many other's lives. She has helped me step into making a positive impact on the world!

Melanie Summers BA
Elem. Ed., MA, C&I and CEO of Innovative Homeschool Solutions™

I met Lady JB Owen shortly after my husband's passing. I decided to write my story of healing through creativity. What I didn't realize at the time was that telling my story would change my life! Lady JB is the perfect muse for my thoughts and feelings—helping to bring out the best, so I can create my own legacy and impact humanity. She is the paintbrush I've filled with colorful imagery and support to help bring my legacy to life!

Kathy Strauss
Creationeer at ImageWerks™ and International Best-selling Author

Lady JB is more than just touching lives; she is changing lives. She has offered sound and creative input in providing advice about business and life. I am thrilled to work with her on the next big step of my journey. I appreciate her integrity and passion in helping me build my legacy.

Andonia Reynolds
InspireNeer and CEO of The Many Hats We Wear

Working with JB has been one of the most amazing experiences in my life and career. She makes finding and showing my best self to others easy and joyful. My only regret is that I didn't find her sooner!

Gina Trimarco
Founder at Carolina Improv Company, Podcast Producer & Host at Women Your Mother Warned You About, Producer & Host at The Pivotal Leader

JB Owen has been nothing short of exceptional. She provided invaluable support, guidance, and encouragement. Her expertise helped me craft a compelling, authentic narrative that resonated deeply with me and my readers.

Dan Gilman
Co-Creative Director at Visual Stream Productions™

Lady JB, you had a vision and made the magic happen. Ignite Humanity has helped me find the light inside, and I am forever grateful. I thank you from the bottom of my heart. Much love and safe travels.

Kari Berridge
Founder of Fit2Motivate™

Working with Lady JB Owen has been an inspiration. The support, caring, nurturing, and high vibes I received have been truly heartwarming. I feel so grateful.

Sharni Quinn
Wellness Expert, Trainer, Speaker and International best-selling author

Lady JB Owen, you are incredible! You've created a legacy and brought together the most loving souls. Thank you for touching my life; I am inspired by you.

Sarah Cross
Founder, Director, and CEO at The Art of Storytelling and International Best-selling Author

Working with Lady JB has been a fabulous experience for me. She is caring, supportive, and smart! What an amazing journey this has been. I'm forever grateful.

Marcia Klostermann
Best Selling Author, "The Warrior Pact"

Thank you, Lady JB, for believing in me, believing in the power to help others heal, and for providing the perfect vehicle for that journey.

MaryAnn Melo
BSc; BEd., and Transformational Coaching of A Gathering of Hearts

I love JB's beautiful energy. I have many other great memories etched into my consciousness from the experience.

Naomi Zion Mark
Company Director, Alternative & Complementary Medicine Practitioner

Lady JB is the most generous person I know.

Nicole Shantel Freeman

Faith Activator, Encouragement Speaker, and Christian Life Coach

Lady JB Owen is a considerate professional.

Karen Louise Wilson

Trainer for The Infinity Life personal development program

Lady JB Owen is amazing!

Stacie Shifflett

Founder & CEO at Modern Consciousness™

Dedication

This book is dedicated to all the people who
have a deep desire to create a legacy, knowing that their effort,
work, and input will make a big difference to humanity.

My heartfelt thanks to the entire Ignite team for your unwavering
support and for being instrumental in making my legacy a reality.

30 ways to
Ignite Your Legacy
in 30 days

> *Legacy is not about leaving something behind, it's about creating something for the future.*

JB Owen

Introduction

Introduction

Congratulations!

By picking up this book, you have taken a powerful and transformative step toward *Igniting Your Legacy.* This moment marks the beginning of a profound journey, one that holds the potential to create lasting change not only in your life, but in the lives of countless others. Your decision to embrace the deeper understanding of making an impact and leaving a meaningful legacy speaks volumes about your commitment to personal growth, self-development, and the betterment of humanity.

Get ready because the journey of creating a legacy will challenge you, inspire you, and ultimately transform you. As you implement the 30 ways suggested here, over the next 30 days, you will delve into the core of who you are, take inspired action toward your mission, and learn the true essence of giving more than what you thought was possible; *that is what legacy is all about.* A deeper commitment to doing more for the good of everyone and a desire to transform in ways that will change lives exponentially.

Your willingness to say "yes" to this journey is a testament to your dedication and desire to make a difference. It's a decision that not everyone makes, but one that holds immense power. By committing to this process, you are not only investing in your personal growth and success but also contributing to the well-being and advancement of those around you.

As you embark on this transformative work, know you are part of a community of like-minded individuals who share your vision and commitment. *Together, we can create a world filled with compassion, inspiration, and amazing experiences.* Your legacy is a gift to future generations, a testament to your devotion, and a willingness to make a meaningful impact that long outlives your time on earth.

The actions you are about to take are not just about personal achievements; they are about understanding the interconnectedness of your decisions and how they shape our world. The steps encouraged here are about realizing that a *true* legacy is built through acts of kindness, generosity, and genuine influence for the good of all. By embracing these key components, you choose to think beyond yourself and prioritize your results for the greater good.

This book and its suggestions are designed to guide you through a series of focused, actionable steps that will help you create a legacy that reflects your authentic nature and allows you to leave a lasting impact on the world we all live in. Throughout these pages, you will find suggestions, strategies, and practical exercises that will help you understand your deepest intentions, set and achieve meaningful goals, and create a ripple effect of positive change. Each day, you will be encouraged to reflect, take action, grow within, and give outwardly. These focused, consistent steps will accumulate into a powerful momentum, propelling you toward the legacy you aspire to create.

Your decision to dedicate your energy to this work is a powerful affirmation of your aspiration to leave a lasting legacy. As you move forward, remember that every decision and action you make contributes to a greater humanity. Your efforts will inspire others, creating a cumulative effect extending far beyond what you can imagine. The work you are about to do will not only transform your life but also leave an indelible mark on the lives of many. Embrace this journey with an open heart and a determined spirit, knowing that you have the power to Ignite your legacy and create a lasting impact that will be felt for generations to come.

Let's get started!

Chapter 1

What Legacy Is Not

*I*n today's fast-paced world, the concept of legacy is often overshadowed by monetary concerns and short-term goals. However, the legacy we leave behind is a *testament* to our life's journey, values, and contributions on a greater scale. Legacy reflects our investment in others and the world around us. Legacy is not just about grand gestures or monumental achievements; it's about the everyday actions and choices collectively shaping our future. Forging a legacy is about understanding who we are, what we stand for, and how we can influence others so that they feel inspired to build a transformative legacy of their own.

Understanding what legacy truly means requires us first to clarify what it is not. Misconceptions about legacy often lead people to chase superficial or temporary markers of success that do little to create lasting impact. By distinguishing these misconceptions, one can better appreciate an effective legacy's profound and enduring nature.

Legacy is not about fame or notoriety. Equating legacy with widespread recognition and media coverage is easy in our celebrity-focused culture. While being well-known can amplify one's impact, fame itself is *not* the marker of legacy. True legacy is measured not by how many people know your name but by how many lives you touch in meaningful ways. It is the quiet teacher who shapes young minds, the community volunteer who tirelessly works for the betterment of others, or the entrepreneur who creates products that improve people's lives by providing lasting solutions. These contributions often go unheralded, yet they form the very bedrock of a *meaningful* legacy.

Furthermore, legacy is not about wealth accumulation. Financial success *can* provide the means to do good, but amassing wealth for its own sake does not constitute a legacy. Wealth can be fleeting and does not necessarily lead to positive change. A true legacy involves using one's resources—whether they be financial, intellectual, or emotional—to uplift and empower others. Legacy Makers are remembered not for their fortunes but for how they used their wealth to address societal challenges and improve atrocities.

Legacy is seldom about personal achievements. Awards, accolades, and personal milestones are gratifying, but they are *not* the sum of one's legacy. Such achievements, while important, are often personal and do not necessarily contribute to the greater good of many. Legacy involves looking beyond personal triumphs to consider how one's *actions benefit a greater collective.* It is about building something that outlasts a single person and continues to benefit people long after one is gone.

Legacy is also not about perfection. Often, people hesitate to pursue legacy-building actions because they feel they must be flawless and pristine. However, legacy is not about being perfect; it is about being authentic and persistent. Mistakes and failures are part of the journey and can enhance one's legacy by building resilience and the willingness to expand and persevere. A real legacy is forged in the process of striving, learning, and continually improving oneself. It is through the pressure and constant force that a diamond is created, similar to the ever-present determination that is involved when designing one's legacy.

Most importantly, legacy is not about control or dominance. Some people mistakenly believe that leaving a legacy means imposing their will or vision on others. True legacy is collaborative and empowering, *not* coercive. It is about inspiring others to carry forward a vision in their own unique way, *not* dictating how it should be done. The most enduring legacies are those that empower others to take ownership of themselves and innovate rather than simply follow a guiding directive.

When we understand that the essence of legacy is what we leave behind for others, not that which we accumulate for ourselves, we shift our focus from seeking recognition or accolades to experiencing the grace and grandness of forming a global legacy. This understanding liberates us from the pressure to conform to societal standards of material success. It allows us to pursue more meaningful and fulfilling paths that promote upliftment for more than just ourselves.

Experiencing the grace that a legacy produces means recognizing the *beauty in selfless actions.* It is about finding joy in giving, mentoring, and supporting others without expecting something in return. When you help a young person find their path, support a colleague in their growth, or contribute to a cause larger than yourself, you create a legacy that transcends individual gratification. The satisfaction derived from more magnanimous actions is profound and enduring, far surpassing the temporary pleasure of individual fulfillment.

I like to believe that the real excitement in developing a legacy lies in its accumulative effect. By focusing on what you can give rather than what you can gain, you create a chain reaction of positive influence. Your actions inspire others to act, creating a multiplying effect that extends your impact far beyond your immediate reach. This is the accurate measure of legacy: not the breadth of your fame or riches, but the *depth and magnitude of a lasting influence.*

When I first contemplated the idea of leaving a lasting impact, I looked to the media and those in the spotlight for inspiration. As I looked beyond the recognition they sought, I began to see the self-serving and financial gain they were seeking. I also saw a parade of self-promotion and fleeting fame. As I continued my search for something more worthy, I discovered stories of *selfless acts of legacy* that seemed to go unnoticed, yet were profoundly impactful.

One such story unfolded in my own town. A single mother, struggling to make ends meet, with little money to take her three young children to play, living in a small, cramped apartment—she found solace in the local playground. Unfortunately, the playground was in dire need of repair and lacked the fun, colorful equipment the other playgrounds had.

Fueled by a fierce determination, she set her sights on a complete renovation. Her mission was to create a new, exciting play area for all the neighborhood children. With unwavering resolve, she embarked on a year-long fundraising campaign. Local businesses, touched by her vision, pledged their support. Parents, yearning for a better play space, rallied behind her.

Her strategy was ingenious. She approached playground manufacturers, offering them advertising and media exposure in exchange for a contribution. She reached out to city officials—the mayor, council members, and constituents garnering their support.

Her tireless efforts paid off. After a year, she had secured $47,000 for the project. On a beautiful June day, the culmination of her dream arrived: the grand unveiling of a state-of-the-art playground, surpassing anything the city had ever seen.

This unveiling was celebrated with a marching band that volunteered their time and a stage built by a local construction company, with all the labor and materials donated. Food trucks showed up to feed everyone; the local radio station was there covering the event and promoting the business supporters. City council members graced the occasion, and the mayor proudly cut the ribbon next to the new monkey bars. Balloons were given out to all the kids, courtesy of the local balloon company, and flowers were gifted to all the moms from the florist around the corner. High school mascots mingled with the crowd, and the local newspaper documented this remarkable story—a testament to how one woman, aspiring to create a legacy for her children, made a massive difference in her community. Her desire was not for herself, but to improve the lives of those she cared about.

By embracing a legacy-focused mindset, one can free oneself of the need for external validation. When your actions are guided by a desire to serve and uplift, you become less concerned with outward approval. This shift in perspective accentuates inner peace and fulfillment, as you derive meaning from the positive change you create rather than from the 'things' you can receive.

Mastering the skills to define a legacy also involves the *humility to recognize that you are part of a larger continuum.* Such an attitude amplifies how important contributions are to a larger cause and the need to improve the greater collective. This perspective puts collaboration and community at the forefront as you build on the work of those who came before you and support those who will continue after you.

Knowing what legacy means helps clarify what it truly is: *a selfless, enduring effort that benefits others and transcends personal agendas.* By understanding the importance of cultivating a legacy, we can experience the joy and emotional rewards that come from it. Building a legacy is uplifting, cultivating, and empowering others— creating a never-ending wave of positivity reverberating throughout all generations.

Chapter 2

Start Your Legacy at Any Age

One of the most pervasive myths about legacy is that it is something to be considered later in life, perhaps when we have achieved a certain level of success or reached a particular milestone. *This notion couldn't be further from the truth.* Legacy is not bound by age; it is defined by the actions we take and the impact we make, *regardless of how old we are.* With inspired action and a driving force, anyone can begin creating their legacy.

Young people, in particular, often underestimate their potential to leave a lasting impact. However, history is filled with examples of young individuals who have made significant contributions to their communities and the world. Take Malala Yousafzai, who, at a young age, became a *global advocate for girls' education,* or Greta Thunberg, who has *mobilized millions to address climate change.* These young leaders demonstrate that age *is not* a barrier to creating meaningful change. The key lies in recognizing your unique passions and talents and channeling them into actions that benefit others. Take, for example, Mahatma Gandhi, who began *leading the Indian independence movement in his 50s*, or Anna Mary Robertson Moses, a celebrated American folk artist who didn't *begin to paint until she was in her late 70s*. Age is just a number, not an indicator of *when* to begin your legacy. Anyone can effectively create a legacy at any age when they bring forth new perspectives, inspire energy, and have a willingness to redefine the status quo.

Starting your legacy means embracing opportunities to make a difference whenever they arise. It could be through volunteer work, community projects, innovative ideas, creative gestures, or simply *by being a positive influence in the lives of those around you.* When you act with intention and a sense of purpose, every small effort contributes to a larger end result. For example, a teenager who starts a recycling initiative at school *not only* improves their local environment *but also* inspires others to adopt sustainable practices. A seasoned entrepreneur who creates a product that solves a common problem *not only* builds a successful business *but also* improves the lives of their customers.

Beginning your legacy right now allows you to grow and evolve as your legacy unfolds and materializes. As you gain experience and insights, your impact widens *and* deepens. Undergoing continuous development ensures that your legacy is not a fixed endpoint but a dynamic, evolving force. By starting, you give yourself the gift of time to refine your vision, learn from your experiences, and create a more profound and lasting impact that develops with you and reflects the person you are maturing into.

Legacy is a living, breathing pursuit that can begin at any time. With honest intentions and an inner willingness, you can establish your legacy now and experience the joy a legacy brings to you at any stage in your life. As you delve into this program, embrace your passions, take intentional steps, and remember that the sooner you start, the more time you have to build, refine, expand, and *enjoy* the legacy you create. Constructing your legacy is an ongoing journey that matures as you do. The key is to seize opportunities, make a difference, and use your unique life experiences to drive your impact at every stage of your life.

You may be questioning if this is the right time to begin your legacy. I hope that choosing to read this book means there is a part of you ready to take the first steps and begin, and you recognize that age is not a factor. What is driving you forward is the feeling you have inside about building your legacy over time and with enthusiasm.

I don't consider myself young, nor am I old either, yet I do consider myself at a stage in my life where working toward a legacy is more meaningful than other aspirations I had in my youth. I see my vivacious spirit and spry attitude as a perfect combination to begin crystallizing my legacy. With a few decades of life experiences under my belt and many more to come, I looked around and realized that there was no time like the present to begin the process of formulating a legacy. Life was not going to slow down and the world was certainly not going to idly wait for me to show up. If I wanted to make a difference in my life and the lives of others I needed to start.

I'll admit I didn't have all the answers, nor an inkling of where to begin. Legacy seemed like a distant place I had yet to reach. Yet, like any big adventure or great quest, forming a legacy starts with a single idea, a grand conviction, a willingness to do more, and a burning desire to take the first step. That mindset and determination did not come with age, it came with *knowing what I wanted*, *believing in what I could do*, and *trusting that my actions would improve not only my life but the lives of many.* This inner knowing, desire to take action, and willingness to give was where I started in my legacy process. I didn't let age be the determining factor, I let the process of getting there be my guide.

Wherever you are in life, let your attitude and ideas inspire your legacy plans. Dip into the emotions, feelings, and wishes for the future and let them guide your choices going forward. Lean into the action you can take right now and adopt the key components I took to drive your journey there. There is no time like the present, and as you begin to build your legacy, before you know it, you will soon see it materializing before your very eyes.

Chapter 3

Adopting the Three Pillars of Legacy

Legacy is a grand and noble endeavor, but the perception that it is inherently complex or unattainable can be a deterrent. I want to demystify legacy-building by breaking down the steps into manageable, enjoyable, replicable actions, and reveal to you the solid, reliable pillars that form viable results. Through my experiences and observations of other legacy makers, I've distilled the essence of legacy creation into three key components: KNOWING, DOING, and GIVING. These pillars have guided my journey and served as a roadmap for achieving what I consider *the heart of legacy manifestation.*

All things with meaning and substance revolve around intrinsic systems or pillars of dependability. Building a legacy is no different; for it to be strong and fortified, it requires a solid foundation and a set of unwavering pillars to support it. These pillars must include values that ensure direction and achievability. Just as a building relies on its structural supports to withstand time and adversity, a legacy relies on core principles to ensure its lasting impact. By establishing and nurturing the foundational elements of KNOWING, DOING, and GIVING, one can create a legacy that is resilient, meaningful, and capable of enduring challenges. As your legacy continues to emanate, each of these fundamental pillars allows you to build *and* achieve more.

To truly Ignite one's legacy, you must immerse yourself in the pillars that form the very foundation of a legacy's principles. You must also integrate the concepts into your decisions, habits, and beliefs— thoughts may need to shift, and awakenings might have to happen for you to actualize the legacy you dream of. To succeed in this you must study the components and learn them by heart. Become curious about how each pillar works and the ways you can integrate them into your life. In adopting the pillars of KNOWING, DOING, and GIVING, you form the foundation of what to build upon as you proceed forward. Each is designed to be simple and yet profound so that they are memorable and fundamental to your legacy-building endeavor.

We are not always taught these pillars via life skills, business ventures, or success strategies. Parental instruction, societal examples, or monetization practices rarely include the pillars of inner work, decisive intentions, or magnanimous generosity. We need to learn these traits and *awaken ourselves to their importance and vitalness.*

To help deepen your understanding of each pillar, I have taken the time to outline their fundamental traits and inherent values. The goal is that in understanding the key components of each pillar, you will spark the desire to incorporate them into a daily practice and automatic way of life. I hope that you begin to use each pillar as a stepping stone to develop your legacy and build a firm foundation of the impact you want to be known for. We all need direction and guidance when doing something new. We *don't know what we don't know* until we learn it. Therefore, be willing to learn something new and incorporate the techniques to help amplify your work. Using the KNOWING, DOING, and GIVING pillars of legacy creation, you will reach your goals sooner—enriched, and with more confidence.

These are the pillars that will bring *your legacy to life!*

Knowing

Chapter 4

Deepening Your Understanding of Legacy

The first pillar in forming a legacy is *KNOWING*. This involves a deep understanding of the essence of who you are and what drives you. Knowing is about *clarifying the core values you draw from, what is most important to you,* and *the unique qualities that define your essence.* Self-awareness forms the foundation upon which your legacy is built and solidifies the *knowing* that you will act upon.

I remember the day vividly when I felt called to act upon my legacy. COVID-19 had been rampant for over a year, and my three teenagers were showing signs of emotional distress, mental fatigue, and personal self-doubt. Each was exhibiting uncertainty and a lack of optimism for their future. It was trying for everyone, but I particularly noticed in them *a fear of the future*, a *worry of the unknown*, and a *dismal attitude* about what was possible.

In a desire to help them, I began to Google™, "Who is igniting humanity? Who is making the upliftment of humanity their legacy?" To my dismay, I found no one. Various references to legacy and humanity appeared, but no individual stood out as leading a movement to shift the conversation toward solving problems and fostering hope on a global scale.

That night, as I went to bed, I felt deeply upset that no one seemed to be making the emotional future of humanity their legacy. Many proposed solutions and ideas, but no one claimed it as their mission. Tossing and turning, frustrated that future generations were not being prioritized and that innovation and resolution were not at the forefront, I grappled with the thought of who would stand up and make a difference.

As I pondered this problem, I was suddenly struck with an absolute knowing: *Igniting Humanity was my responsibility.* I felt, with every fiber of my being, that I could no longer complain or wish for someone else to make it important. It was up to me to make uplifting humanity *my* legacy.

No one needed to tell me to do it; I just knew it from my core. I felt it in my soul and with the very fiber of my being. I completely understood within myself and the world around me that I must focus my time and energies on building a legacy that would indeed *Ignite Humanity*.

That direct and earnest knowing was the spark that started the flame that burned the embers of a legacy I work at to this very day. That devotion and conviction that came from within was the catalyst that inspired my thoughts and actions going forward. When you know your purpose and are clear on the mission you wish to create, your legacy will be revealed and shown to you. I learned immediately that *knowing* is the first step in building one's legacy.

The Knowing Within Legacy

As you delve into your *knowing,* you will begin to understand your competencies, strengths, and passions. You'll be more introspective and reflective, helping you to identify what truly matters to you and what you want to be remembered for. *Knowing* is the foundation upon which you can build a legacy that is authentic and aligned with your true self.

As I mentor others on building their legacy I emphasize the importance of self-discovery and inner knowingness. Legacy starts with self-reflection—identifying your passions, values, and the unique contributions you can make to the world. It's about understanding what you stand for and what you *wish to leave behind.* Knowing your innate essence allows you to create a legacy that is deeply rooted in your internal *why* and sacred identity.

To fully *know* requires activities and exercises that encourage self-discovery. These may include journaling prompts, personality assessments, and reflective practices that help you gain clarity on your purpose and goals. By deepening your understanding of yourself, you can make more intentional choices that resonate with your inner values and overall vision for your legacy.

I encourage you to reflect on your values, essence, and passions; consider what excites you and what you believe in wholeheartedly. The *knowing* process isn't about achieving but, instead, gaining clarity on what matters most to you. When you align your actions with your beliefs, your legacy becomes a natural extension of who you are, and you tend to naturally gravitate toward what direction you must take and what goals you want to achieve. Your knowingness guides your convictions and directs your actions from a deeper place of meaning and self-assurance.

Working on one's *knowing* is not what others might suggest when it comes to building a legacy, yet it is a key component and a fundamental pillar in the overall process. *Knowing* is an integral factor and becomes the flint that sparks the flame that will keep your conviction going when you feel the urge to quit. The following key elements expand upon the essence of *knowing* and share why this pillar is so imperative and essential to foster and cultivate.

The Essence of Inner Knowing

Inner knowing is the profound sense of self-awareness and intuition that guides your actions and decisions. It is the inner compass that aligns your life with your true values and purpose. This intrinsic understanding of oneself is not merely a passive state of Being but an active, dynamic process of self-discovery and growth. By tapping into your inner knowing, you gain clarity about *who you are, what you stand for, and the unique contributions you can make to the world.*

Cultivating Inner Knowing

Cultivating inner knowing involves incorporating practices such as mindfulness, reflection, and active listening to your inner voice. These practices help you to tune out external noise and distractions, allowing you to connect with your authentic self. Visualization, meditation, and spending time in nature can also facilitate this deeper inner connection. As you become more attuned to your inner knowing, you begin to *trust* your instincts and make decisions that resonate with your true self.

The Connection to Inner Knowing

A lasting legacy is deeply rooted in the authenticity that comes from inner knowing. When you are aligned with your true self, your actions are more likely to be heartfelt and selfless. This deeper-rooted alignment ensures that the legacy you build is a *true reflection* of your core values and beliefs. People are naturally drawn to authenticity, and a legacy built on such a foundation is more likely to inspire and resonate with others, leaving a lasting impact.

Chapter 5

Self—Assurance in Building Legacy

*I*f you feel that *knowing* is intangible and hard to measure or locate, let *self-assurance* be the driving force and litmus test. *Self-assurance* is rooted in actions, behaviors, thoughts, and opinions. It manifests in the confidence with which you approach your goals, the steadfastness in your decisions, and your resilience in the face of challenges. Your own *self-assurance* will help fuel the fire within you to reach your objectives, acting as a catalyst for perseverance and determination. When you are *self-assured*, you are more likely to take decisive actions, maintain a positive outlook, and stay committed to your vision. This inner confidence propels you forward and inspires a belief within yourself. *Self-assurance* becomes a powerful force, enabling you to overcome obstacles and silence the critics. Ultimately, *self-assurance* lays the groundwork for building a lasting legacy by ensuring that your efforts are driven by an unwavering *knowing* of yourself and your potential.

*Self-assuranc*e is vital to building your legacy because it serves as the foundation for the perseverance and resilience you will require. When you are confident in your abilities and vision, you can navigate the inevitable challenges and setbacks with determination and clarity. *Self-assurance* fuels the belief that your efforts will make a meaningful impact, allowing you to stay focused on your goals despite external doubts and criticisms. This inner confidence not only inspires you to follow your vision but also reinforces your commitment to your mission, ensuring that your legacy is built on a solid and unwavering belief in your purpose and potential.

When I awoke the next day after I felt my *inner knowing*, resolute in my decision to build a legacy of Igniting Humanity, my first order of business was to envision my goal, trust it was *for* me, and feel it already happening and beautifully complete. I had to be self-assured that it *could* be done. No one was going to do it for me; some would likely doubt me, and many would say it couldn't be achieved. I had to resist allowing the naysayers and critics to persuade me otherwise. If I was going to fulfill my destiny and create my legacy, I had to believe in myself with complete faith, trust, and a genuine knowing of *self-assurance* that I would not waver; no matter what.

Self-assurance is the confidence in your abilities and the belief in your potential to achieve your goals. It is the unwavering trust in yourself that empowers you to take uninhibited actions and pursue your inspired dreams. This sense of confidence is not about being arrogant or infallible but about having a realistic and self-assured view of your capabilities and worth.

Strengthening Your Inner Knowing

To strengthen your *inner knowing*, it is essential to engage in continuous self-reflection and personal growth. Seek feedback from trusted friends and mentors, and be open to new experiences that challenge your perspectives. Embrace the journey of self-discovery, knowing that it is a lifelong process. As you deepen your understanding of yourself, you will find that your ability to create a meaningful and lasting legacy will naturally follow.

Building Self-Assurance

Building self-assurance requires a combination of self-assessment, self-reflection, and self-guidance. Start by recognizing your strengths and achievements, and use them as a foundation for confidence, knowing, and discernment. Continuously develop your skills and knowledge to enhance your competence and proficiency. Embrace failures and setbacks as opportunities for learning and growth, building resilience, appreciation, and self-discovery in the face of adversity.

The Impact Self-Assurance Makes

Self-assurance plays a crucial role in building a lasting legacy. When you believe in yourself, you are more likely to take risks, pursue ambitious goals, and persevere through obstacles. This determination and courage inspires others and sets a powerful example. A legacy built on *self-assurance* reflects the strength and conviction of such a person, making it more likely to *endure and persevere*.

Examples of Self-Assured Legacy Builders

History is filled with examples of individuals who leveraged their *self-assurance* to create lasting legacies. Consider the story of a scientist who, despite facing skepticism and opposition, persisted in their research because they *believed* in its potential impact. Their self-assurance drove them to make groundbreaking discoveries that transformed their field and left a lasting legacy of innovation and progress.

- **Nelson Mandela's** *self-assurance* was pivotal in his fight against apartheid in South Africa. Despite being imprisoned for 27 years, *Mandela never wavered in his belief in justice and equality.* His confidence in the righteousness of his cause inspired millions, and ultimately led to the dismantling of apartheid and the establishment of a democratic South Africa. Mandela's legacy of resilience, leadership, and unwavering commitment to human rights continues to *inspire people around the world.*

- **Marie Curie's** groundbreaking work in radioactivity exemplifies *self-assurance* in the face of adversity. Despite the significant gender biases of her time, Curie pursued her scientific research with unwavering confidence in her abilities. Her discoveries earned her *two Nobel Prizes in Physics and Chemistry*, making her the first person to win Nobel Prizes in two different scientific fields. Curie's legacy of scientific excellence and perseverance continues to influence and inspire future generations of scientists.

- **Steve Jobs,** the co-founder of Apple Inc.™, is renowned for his visionary leadership and *self-assurance.* His confidence in his innovative ideas, even when they were unconventional or ahead of their time, drove him to create products that revolutionized technology and consumer electronics. Jobs' legacy is reflected in the lasting impact of Apple's products and the company's continued influence on technology, design, and media. His story is a testament to the power of self-belief and determination to achieve extraordinary success.

- **Rosa Parks'** self-assured stand against racial segregation made her an enduring symbol of the Civil Rights Movement. Park's act of defiance in 1955, when she refused to give up her seat on a bus to a white passenger, sparked the *Montgomery Bus Boycott*. Her confidence in her right to equality and her courageous actions played a significant role in the fight against racial discrimination in the United States. Park's legacy lives on as a testament to the power of individual courage and determination in effecting social change.

Fostering Self-Assurance

To foster *self-assurance*, surround yourself with supportive and encouraging people who *believe* in your potential. Set achievable goals and celebrate your successes along the way. Engage in activities that challenge you and push you out of your comfort zone—these experiences build confidence and resilience. Practice self-compassion and maintain a positive mindset, focusing on your growth and progress rather than perfection.

I have to admit that igniting humanity is *no small goal*, and when I first shared my vision, a few of the people I love most responded with the proverbial raised eyebrow. They thought it was outlandish, too grand, and even downright impossible to achieve. Some didn't offer their support, and others may have secretly wanted me to fail. This skepticism and doubt could have easily derailed me, but instead, I chose to shift my focus. I understood that to bring my vision to life, I needed to surround myself with those who genuinely believed in me and my mission, even if I fell short of my ultimate goal.

Igniting humanity was a monumental task, but I firmly believed that if I aimed high, followed my dreams, worked tirelessly, and stayed focused, I would achieve something meaningful. Even if my efforts didn't reach all of humanity, touching the lives of some would still be a remarkable accomplishment. This mindset helped me stay resilient in the face of doubt and criticism.

Surrounding yourself with people who want to see you succeed is crucial. These are the individuals who will lift you up when you're down, encourage you when you're doubtful, and celebrate your victories, *no matter how small*. They provide the support and motivation needed to keep striving toward your goals.

I encourage you to aim high with your goals and fill your life with people who want to see you reach whatever you set out to achieve. These are the people who will stand by you, believe in you, and help you turn your dreams into a reality.

As you embark on your journey to building a lasting legacy, remember that it begins with a deep understanding of yourself and a *strong belief in your abilities*. Cultivate your inner knowing and *self-assurance* through continuous self-reflection, personal growth, and embracing challenges. By aligning your actions with your authentic self and confidently pursuing your goals, you create a legacy that reflects your true values and has a *lasting impact on the world.* Embrace this journey with passion and purpose, knowing that you have the power to shape a better future for yourself and others.

Chapter 6

Knowing & Self-Assurance

Inner knowing and *self-assurance*, when integrated, create a powerful foundation for building a lasting legacy. *Inner knowing* provides a deep, intuitive understanding of one's values, passions, and purpose. It is the internal compass that guides decisions and actions. *Self-assurance,* on the other hand, is the confidence and belief in one's abilities to achieve goals and overcome challenges. When these two elements are harmonized, they form a dynamic force that drives meaningful and impactful actions to form true conviction.

Integrating *inner knowing* and *self-assurance* begins with aligning your values with your actions. Inner knowing helps you identify what truly matters to you, what you stand for, and what you wish to contribute to the world. Self-assurance gives you the confidence to act on these insights, pursue your passions, and make decisions that reflect your core values. This alignment ensures that your efforts are authentic and resonate deeply with both *yourself* and *others.*

Self-assurance is crucial in overcoming doubts and challenges that inevitably arise on the path to building a legacy. When you are deeply connected to your *inner knowing*, you are more resilient in the face of obstacles because you are driven by a strong sense of purpose. *Self-assurance* empowers you to face these challenges head-on, believing in your capacity to navigate difficulties and emerge stronger. This combination of inner clarity and external confidence enables you to persevere and stay committed to your vision.

Integrating *inner knowing* with *self-assurance* fosters authentic leadership. Authentic leaders inspire others through their achievements and genuine commitment to their values with confidence in their vision. When you lead with both self-awareness and *self-assurance*, you create a positive and inspiring environment. People are drawn to leaders who are true to themselves and confident in their mission, making it easier to mobilize support and drive collective efforts toward meaningful goals.

A legacy built on the integration of *inner knowing* and *self-assurance* is dynamic and adaptable. Inner knowing encourages continuous self-reflection and personal growth, ensuring that your actions remain aligned with your evolving values and insights. *Self-assurance* provides the courage to embrace change, take risks, and adapt to new circumstances. This adaptability is crucial for sustaining a lasting impact, as it allows your legacy to evolve and remain relevant in a forever changing world.

Ways to Foster Your Knowing

1. **Regular reflection**: Set aside time to regularly reflect on your values, passions, and goals. Journaling, meditation, and spending time in nature can help deepen your connection to your inner knowing.

2. **Seek feedback**: Engage with trusted friends, mentors, and colleagues to gain insights and perspectives that can enhance your self-awareness and confidence.

3. **Set aligned goals**: Ensure that your goals are aligned with your core values and passions. This alignment will make it easier to stay motivated and committed.

4. **Celebrate achievements**: Acknowledge and celebrate your successes, no matter how small. This practice boosts your self-assurance and reinforces your belief in your abilities.

5. **Embrace challenges**: View challenges as opportunities for growth. Trust in your capacity to overcome obstacles and learn from each experience.

6. **Stay authentic**: Always act in a way that is true to yourself. Authenticity builds trust and credibility, which are essential for a lasting legacy.

I make a point of reviewing these six steps continuously to ensure I am always increasing my connection to my *'knowingness'* and solidifying the foundation to stay convicted of my goal. Integrating *knowing* into your life is a powerful principle when it comes to building a lasting legacy. When we *know,* we feel connected to who we are at an intrinsic level. This emboldens our decisions, passions, and the contributions we choose to make. *Knowing* is about connecting with your inner self and drawing from your greatest source. When you have a clear sense of your true *knowing*, you can align your actions with what matters most, creating a legacy that is effective and meaningful.

Connecting to your *knowing* is an intentional process and one that is addressed in the first section of this book. Use the various methods suggested here to find your *knowing* and activate it. If you find connecting with your inner knowing challenging consider coming to a class I give each week called *Ignite Inspires*, designed to help you discover the inner part of you that yearns to be expressed. I often call this class *the roadmap to your greatness*. If you are interested in attending, just reach out to support@igniteyou.life and we will send you a personal invite. It's 100% FREE!

Finding your *inner knowing* is not an overnight revelation but a gradual and deeply personal journey. It requires time, introspection, and a willingness to explore the depths of your soul. Patience is crucial in this process, as the path to self-awareness and clarity is often filled with periods of uncertainty. Recognizing that this journey is not linear, but rather a continuous evolution can help you stay committed to discovering your true self.

Self-discovery involves confronting both your strengths and vulnerabilities, and this can be challenging all alone. Embrace self-compassion and understand that experiencing setbacks is a natural part of growth. Each step you take contributes to understanding who you are and what you stand for. That means the *process* of finding your inner knowing is what matters most. It is through this journey that you develop the insights, wisdom, and resilience needed to build and conceptualize your legacy. As you engage in the practices outlined here, you will enhance your self-awareness, uncover your values, and unearth the passion and purposes that define your visionary expression. This ongoing exploration strengthens your connection to your knowing and enriches your life in exponential ways.

Be patient and supportive toward yourself during this journey as this will allow you to fully embrace the transformative experiences that lead to self-discovery. Cherish the victories and blessings learned along the way, knowing that each moment of clarity and self-awareness brings you *closer to your true calling.* By nurturing yourself with kindness and self-acceptance, you create a fertile ground for your *inner knowing* to flourish, ultimately guiding you toward a legacy that will forever make you proud.

Doing

Chapter 7

Taking Inspired Actions

The second pillar required to create a legacy is *DOING*. Being aware of your essence and knowing your values are crucial, but without taking action and doing something, nothing gets accomplished. Legacy-building requires taking tangible steps toward your goals. It's about putting in the time, effort, and dedication to master the mechanics yourself. *No one can create your legacy for you; it is a personal journey that demands your active participation and dedicated attention.*

When you focus on *doing* you can translate your insights and understandings into tangible tasks. It's not enough to know what you *want* to achieve; you must also take deliberate steps to *make* them happen. *Doing* is about setting goals, creating action plans, and developing the habits and disciplines necessary to turn your aspirations into a reality.

Doing also means exploring various strategies for effective goal setting, time management, and productivity. You must learn how to break down your big visions into manageable tasks, and how to stay motivated and accountable to reach the finish line. By consistently taking inspired actions, you will build momentum and make steady progress toward creating the markers of your legacy. With all action comes results—meaning one must work toward the results they seek.

Throughout my journey, I've realized that action is mandatory. From publishing authors around the globe, building eco-friendly and sustainable brands and products, and raising funds for schools in impoverished countries—every achievement required decisive action. My steps were about transforming ideas and values into concrete deeds. Whether it's starting a new project, volunteering, mentoring, or any other form of contribution; action is what turns aspirations into reality.

When I decided to help authors share their stories with the world, I knew that envisioning such a goal was *just the beginning.* Every manuscript that landed on my desk was a dream waiting to be realized. It wasn't enough to appreciate the potential in their stories; I had to act. This meant long hours of editing, coordinating with printers, and organizing book launches. Each book published was a testament to the power of action—taking an idea, nurturing it, and bringing it to life on printed pages.

My commitment to sustainability didn't stop at recognizing its importance. I had to take concrete steps to build brands and products that were not only eco-friendly but also viable in the marketplace. This involved rigorous research, product development, and establishing supply chains that adhered to commercial standards. It was a journey of countless meetings, trials, and iterations. Yet, each step forward was driven by the belief that real change comes from *doing*, not just dreaming.

Raising funds for schools in impoverished countries was another area where action was imperative. The vision of providing education to children who lacked access was noble, but it required tangible efforts to become a reality. Organizing fundraising events, reaching out to donors, collaborating with local communities, and even cycling on a tandem bike with my husband 10,000 kilometers across Canada to raise awareness *were all part of the process.* Each donation we received supported our cause and was a direct result of persistent action and continued movement.

Throughout all of these endeavors, the common thread was *doing*. It wasn't enough to have great ideas and strong values; *I needed to take decisive action to implement them.* Starting a new project involved meticulous planning and relentless execution. Volunteering meant dedicating time and energy to causes I cared about. Mentoring requires patience and a willingness to guide others. In every instance, it was *action* that bridged the gap between aspiration and formulating my legacy.

Moving from Knowing to Doing

Inner knowing lays at the foundation of your legacy, but *action* is what builds it. Transitioning from a mental understanding to tangible results involves setting clear goals and creating a plan to achieve them. It's not enough to have a vision; you must be willing to put in the work to bring that vision to life. This means breaking down your goals into *manageable steps and consistently taking action toward them.*

Taking action is the cornerstone of building a legacy. It's through your actions that you turn your vision into reality and create a lasting impact. By setting attainable goals, staying committed, and embracing the process, you can achieve great things. Remember, your legacy is built one step at a time, through the consistent efforts and the actions you take every day.

There is immense satisfaction in seeing the tangible results of your efforts. Each milestone you achieve, no matter how small, is a testament to your hard work and fortitude. This sense of accomplishment fuels your motivation and reinforces your commitment to your goals. It is from taking action that *more action* is inspired, and that action opens the doors for more actions to materialize.

The Power of Incremental Progress

Building a legacy doesn't happen overnight; it's the result of taking action with incremental efforts. Each small action you take contributes to the larger goal. Achieving progress is about deconstructing your overarching goal into smaller, more manageable tasks. By focusing on completing these smaller tasks one at a time, you steadily move closer to your ultimate objective. This method not only reduces the feeling of being overwhelmed but also provides a clear roadmap for achieving your larger goal—it's a strategy that builds momentum, where each completed task reinforces your confidence and commitment to the next step.

There are many benefits to taking incremental steps to achieve your legacy. *Each step increases sustainability and becomes exactly what you need to Ignite the stage in the process.* One of the most powerful lessons I've learned is the *significance* of small steps. Building a legacy doesn't require grand gestures all the time; often, it's the small, consistent actions that make the most significant difference. Whether it's daily efforts to reduce waste in my sustainable brands, regular mentoring sessions with aspiring authors, or ongoing fundraising activities for schools, these small steps accumulated into substantial progress toward my legacy.

The power of incremental progress lies in its ability to transform daunting goals into achievable, plausible steps. By embracing this approach, you make the process of building a legacy more manageable for yourself. Stay consistent, celebrate your progress, and keep your long-term vision in mind. Through steady, incremental progress, *you will* create a legacy that is meaningful, impactful, and enduring.

Benefits of Incremental Progress

1. **Sustained motivation**: Achieving small milestones regularly keeps you motivated. Each success, no matter how minor, provides a sense of accomplishment that fuels your drive to continue.

2. **Builds confidence**: As you achieve each small goal, your confidence in your abilities grows. This confidence is crucial for tackling more significant challenges and pursuing bigger goals.

3. **Reduces overwhelm**: Breaking down a large goal into smaller tasks makes it less intimidating. It's easier to focus on and complete a single step than to contemplate the entire journey at once.

4. **Continuous improvement**: Incremental progress allows for continuous learning and improvement. Each step provides an opportunity to refine your skills and strategies, leading to better outcomes over time.

5. **Adaptability**: Small, incremental steps make it easier to adjust your approach as needed. If a particular strategy isn't working, you can pivot without having invested too much in a single, large effort.

While incremental progress focuses on short-term actions, it's essential to keep your long-term vision in mind—each small step should align with your broader goals and *contribute* to your legacy. This alignment ensures that your efforts are purposeful and directed toward creating a lasting impact. By balancing short-term actions with a long-term vision, you maintain a clear sense of direction and purpose.

As part of my humanitarian efforts to Ignite Humanity™, I decided to undertake something monumental for my 50th birthday and bring awareness to my cause. Having never ridden a bike extensively, not being an athlete, and just turning 50, I proposed an ambitious plan to my husband: we would ride our tandem bicycle 5,000 kilometers across Canada to raise awareness for our initiative.

I had never ridden a bike that far, lived on the road, traveled through five provinces, or spent 7-9 hours cycling on a small leather seat. We trained for a few weeks in the cold Canadian springtime, venturing out 30 to 40 kilometers each day as practice. When the time came for the big ride, we needed to cover 100 to 150 kilometers each day to reach our goal.

Unfazed by the magnitude of the task, I broke down the overall distance into daily achievements. Each day's ride was divided into three segments: morning, afternoon, and evening, each covering around 40 kilometers. I further broke down each segment into 10-kilometer increments, followed by a break, 20 kilometers with a snack, then another 10 kilometers and a rest before the next set. Within each 10 or 20 kilometers, I focused on the next landmark: the next fence post, road sign, hill, or shady spot. I even broke that down to ten pedal turns at a time, then ten more, or cycling the duration of one song on my headset, and then the next.

After 56 days, my husband and I triumphantly reached the Parliament building in Ottawa, having cycled 5,000 kilometers, one incremental step at a time. This journey was not just a physical feat but *a testament to the power of breaking down big goals into manageable steps.* It was a powerful reminder that monumental achievements are possible with determination, perseverance, and a clear vision one step at a time.

My ride across Canada was more than a personal milestone; it was a symbol of what is possible when we commit to a cause greater than ourselves. It highlighted the importance of raising awareness for our initiative to Ignite Humanity, demonstrating that with dedication and incremental progress, we can achieve extraordinary things. This experience reinforced my belief that each of us has the power to ignite change, one step, one pedal turn, and one legacy ambition at a time.

As you tackle parts of your legacy that may seem daunting, shift your perspective to see how you can reach the finish line through deliberate incremental actions in a more systemized way. For example...

- **Writing a Book** is a monumental task, but it can be accomplished through incremental progress. Instead of focusing on completing the entire manuscript, break it down into chapters, sections, or even daily word count goals. By consistently writing a few pages each day, you gradually build up your manuscript. Over time, these small, daily efforts accumulate into a complete book.

- **Starting a Business** involves numerous steps, from market research and product development to marketing and sales. Instead of trying to tackle everything at once, focus on one aspect at a time. Start with a business plan, then move on to developing a prototype, followed by market testing, and so on. Each completed step brings you closer to your goal of launching a thriving business.

- **Giving Back** can start with small initiatives. Organize a local cleanup day, start a recycling program at your school, or volunteer at a local shelter. Each of these actions contributes to the larger goal of improving your community. Over time, these small efforts can grow into significant, lasting change.

Challenges are inevitable, but incremental progress equips you with the resilience to overcome them. When faced with a setback, the impact is minimized because your efforts are distributed across many small steps. You can quickly adapt and find alternative paths without losing sight of your overall goal. This adaptability ensures that obstacles don't derail your journey but become part of the learning process.

Chapter 8

Legacy Comes From Consistency

Consistency is the backbone of *doing* things with incremental progress. It's not enough to take one small step sporadically; the key is to maintain a regular, sustained effort. This means showing up every day, putting in the work, and staying committed to your goals, even when progress seems slow. Consistency builds habits, and habits are what drive long-term success.

Consistency and dedication are key components of *doing*. Achieving a legacy is not about sporadic efforts but about *sustained action over time.* Dedication means committing to your goals and persevering even when faced with obstacles. It's about showing up every day, putting in the effort, and continuously striving to make progress. This consistent effort is what *transforms ideas into reality* and *dreams into lasting achievements.*

If you have never used the process of incremental actions before, get ready to experience something game-changing. Most of the people who have reached legacy status can attest that this method was used to help them reach their goals. Many who have achieved big endeavors started with these simple rules for doing things in an incremental and obtainable way.

Practical Steps for Taking Action

1. **Set Clear, Achievable Goals**: Define what you want to accomplish in clear, specific terms. Break your goals down into smaller, actionable steps that you can tackle one at a time.

2 **Create a Plan**: Develop a detailed plan outlining the steps you need to take to achieve your goals. Include timelines, resources needed, and potential challenges.

3. **Take Initiative**: Don't wait for the perfect moment or for someone else to give you permission. Start taking action now, even if it's just a small step.

4. **Stay Committed**: Keep your goals in focus and stay committed to the process. Remind yourself of your reasons for pursuing your legacy and use them as motivation.

5. **Adapt and Adjust**: Be flexible and willing to adjust your plan as needed. Challenges and setbacks are part of the journey; learn from them and keep moving forward.

Looking back, I see that my legacy is built on a foundation of consistent incremental steps. Each book published, product created, and school funded was a part of doing things in small, obtainable steps that led to the grand plan. Working this way is a reminder that *our actions today shape the world of tomorrow.* By taking decisive steps consistently and committing to meaningful actions, we can all create lasting legacies that reflect our values and commitment.

When clients come to me to be mentored in their legacy, I always assess not just their mental mindset, but also their consistency in effort and dedication to *doing*. One must be innovative, malibible, and fervent. That means being adaptable to changes, willing to pivot and adjust, but also unwavering and committed to taking consistent action and not giving up. As I work with my clients further, I make sure to address the important aspects of doing and not getting lost in the feeling of overwhelm. I've also encouraged them to embrace the process, understanding that every action, no matter how small, contributes to the larger picture. It's about being present and fully engaged in each step, appreciating the journey as much as the destination. The satisfaction of seeing a project come to fruition is immense, but so is the joy of knowing that through actively doing one is making a difference every day.

The power of continuous effort and dedication cannot be overstated. It's through persistent action, small steps, and unwavering commitment that we build a legacy that stands the test of time. Each day is an opportunity to take action, make progress, and move closer to your goals. Embrace the journey, celebrate your achievements, and stay dedicated to your vision. Your legacy is the sum of your daily efforts, and through consistent, meaningful action, you can create a lasting impact that inspires and empowers all humanity.

To ensure your daily actions align with a *doing* mentality, here is a list of behaviors and habits you can add to your daily routine.

The Hands-On Approach to Legacy

If you look at any great legacy you will see that the *doing* came from the people connected to the goal. Building a legacy requires mastering the mechanics yourself. It's about actively participating in every step of the process and taking full responsibility for the outcome. When you immerse yourself in the work, you gain a deeper understanding and appreciation of what it takes to achieve the goal. This active involvement means you are *directly shaping the outcome*, ensuring that your legacy is a product of your hard work and dedication, not contingent on someone else. It's not enough to have a vision; you must be the one to bring it to life through consistent effort and attention to detail. Every decision, action, and adjustment is an opportunity to infuse your personal touch and unique perspective into the legacy you are building.

While guidance and support from others are valuable and can provide crucial insights and encouragement, the core work must come from you. Relying solely on others can dilute the authenticity and personal significance of your legacy. By taking a hands-on approach, you ensure that your legacy truly reflects your values, vision, and efforts. This personal involvement solidifies your commitment and builds resilience and confidence as you navigate challenges and celebrate milestones. Ultimately, a legacy that you have crafted through your own efforts is more meaningful and enduring, resonating deeply with both yourself and those impacted by your work.

Learning and Skill Development

One of the key aspects of working toward your legacy is continuous learning and skill development. As you manifest your goals, *acquiring the knowledge and skills needed to succeed becomes imperative.* This journey might involve formal education, such as enrolling in courses or pursuing degrees that enhance your understanding and capabilities in your chosen field. Training programs and workshops offer specialized skills directly applicable to your projects, providing hands-on experience and practical insights. Additionally, self-directed learning plays a crucial role, allowing you to explore areas of interest at your own pace and delve deeply into subjects that align with your directive. This multifaceted approach to learning ensures that you are well-equipped to tackle the challenges and seize the opportunities that will enhance your legacy.

By investing in your development, you equip yourself with the tools necessary to achieve your goals. This investment goes beyond mere knowledge acquisition; it involves cultivating a growth mindset that embraces continuous improvement and adaptability. As you expand your skill set, you become more versatile, resilient, and able to navigate the evolving landscape of your endeavors. Each new skill learned and each piece of knowledge gained adds to your arsenal, empowering you to innovate and excel.

The Importance of Practice and Persistence

Practice is essential in mastering any skill or achieving any goal. It's through repeated efforts and persistence that you improve and refine your abilities. Whether it's honing a craft, developing a leadership mindset, or building a conglomerate, consistent practice is crucial. Persistence means continuing to put in the effort, even when progress is slow or challenges arise. Practice means continuing to perfect your skills no matter how much you believe you know.

The journey of building a legacy is not without its setbacks. I've faced challenges and failures along the way, but each setback has been an opportunity to learn and grow. Instead of viewing failures as insurmountable obstacles, I've learned to see them as valuable lessons to hone my skills and keep working toward the next milestone. Each failure has taught me something new, helping me *refine* my approach and improve my strategies. I recognize all setbacks as a way to practice more of *who I need to be* to reach my goal.

Building a Support System

While the primary responsibility for building your legacy rests with you, having a support system can be incredibly helpful. Surround yourself with people who believe in your vision and can provide encouragement, advice, and assistance. This support system can include mentors, peers, family, and friends. Their insights and encouragement can help you stay motivated and navigate obstacles.

I am proud to say the IGNITE community is a collection of enviable people, all dedicated to igniting others and uplifting humanity. Any one of the people in the Ignite ecosystem would be delighted to help you reach your goals. You can meet them on our Facebook page: @*Ignite You* or @*Ignite Your Frequency* and at many of our events, summits, and book launches; just google Gatherama, Ignitearama, or Ignite Publishing™. You will be amazed at the assistance you get and the beneficial supporting system you'll be a part of.

Taking Responsibility

Taking responsibility for your legacy means owning your actions and their outcomes. It's about being accountable for the steps you take and the progress you make. This sense of ownership drives you to be proactive and diligent in your efforts. When you take responsibility, *you are more likely to stay committed and see your goals through to completion.*

Dedication is the unwavering commitment to your goals and values. It's about showing up every day, even when *the going gets tough*. Dedication means persevering through challenges, staying focused on the vision, and consistently putting in the effort required to make a difference. It's this dedication that transforms dreams into reality and creates a legacy that endures.

Embracing Challenges and Adaptability

Challenges are an inevitable part of the journey to building a legacy. Embracing these challenges with a positive mindset and a willingness to adapt is essential. Adaptability means being open to change and adjusting your plans as needed. You can overcome obstacles and continue moving forward by staying flexible and resilient.

Persistent adaptability has a ripple effect, influencing others and inspiring them to take action. When people see the tangible results of your efforts to overcome difficulties, they are motivated to contribute and join the cause. This collective effort amplifies the impact, creating a legacy that extends beyond your individual contributions and makes challenges seem less daunting and manageable.

Overcoming the Fear of Failure

Fear of failure is a common barrier to taking action. It's important to recognize that *failure is not the opposite of success, but a part of the process.* Each failure provides valuable lessons that help you grow and improve. Embrace failure as an opportunity to learn and refine your approach rather than a reason to give up.

Mastering the mechanics of legacy building is a journey that requires overcoming the fears around limiting beliefs, pessimism, and not feeling good enough. By taking a hands-on approach, investing in yourself, and embracing your talents, you create a legacy that will persevere, diminishing failure. Each step you take, each skill you develop, and each challenge you overcome contributes to the legacy you leave behind. Embrace the process, take responsibility, and enjoy the satisfaction of building something meaningful and enduring.

There is no time limit, perfect scenario, or people keeping score. Your legacy is your process, and through decisive action and knowing yourself, you can abolish fears and make failure non-existent.

Celebrating Small Wins

Celebrating small wins is crucial in the journey of legacy building. *Recognize and reward yourself for each milestone achieved, no matter how small.* This positive reinforcement keeps you motivated and acknowledges the effort you've put in, as well as providing a moment to reflect on your progress and appreciate how far you've come. Celebrate your progress along the way and acknowledge the effort you're putting in—positive reinforcement will keep you motivated and encourage you to continue taking action.

Celebrating progress, no matter how small, has been essential in maintaining motivation and enthusiasm. It's easy to get caught up in the long-term vision and forget to appreciate the milestones achieved along the way. Taking time to acknowledge and celebrate these achievements provides a sense of accomplishment and *fuels the drive to keep going.*

Chapter 9

Every Win Counts

I'll admit that deciding to cycle across the vast expanse of Canada brought up numerous challenges related to fear, support, responsibility, adaptability, and persistence. That journey continuously tested each of these qualities. It was an endless *ebb and flow* of navigating obstacles, overcoming roadblocks, and dealing with extreme weather, wilderness, and communication issues. Despite the difficulties, *I wouldn't change a single thing.* Every challenge was precisely what we needed to experience in order to learn and prevail, propelling us to the next section of our trip.

We had to endure all of that to *emerge triumphant.* Despite the sore muscles, tender backsides, sunburned skin, and numerous bike repairs, it was one of the most rewarding and uplifting experiences I've ever had. In doing so, I not only uplifted my own life but also inspired thousands of others who followed our journey online. People supported our cause and saw our unwavering commitment, which inspired them to create their own legacies. Hundreds shared how our actions motivated them to take action, sparking many others to pursue their own dreams and make a difference.

That journey across Canada was not just a physical endeavor but a profound testament to human resilience and the ripple effect of inspiration. It demonstrated that with determination and perseverance, we can overcome any obstacle and ignite a movement that touches countless lives.

What made the journey so impactful was that each day we celebrated our riding wins. It could have been a huge day covering over 100 kilometers, a daunting hill of only 50 kilometers, a rain-filled afternoon that washed out our riding, or a breathtaking sunset across a lake that took our breath away. Regardless of the distance, we celebrated our successes and each day and shared our genuine experience with our followers our genuine experience. We showed them that it isn't about the numbers you achieve; *it's about the impact you make and the attitude you take*. By sharing our daily victories, no matter how small, we demonstrated that every step forward counts and that the journey itself is what truly matters.

I encourage you to take daily action toward building your legacy. Through hard work, practice, perseverance, and responsibility, celebrate both the big and small wins along the way. Recognize where you are making a difference, one step at a time, and use the many qualities of legacy-making to guide you to the finish line of reaching your dreams. Each action, no matter how small, brings you closer to achieving your goals and making a lasting impact.

Lessons Learned from Taking Action

1. **Clarity through action**: Taking the first step often brings clarity that planning alone cannot provide. Each action taken illuminates the path forward, revealing new opportunities and insights.

2. **Building momentum**: Action creates momentum. Once you start moving toward your goal, each subsequent step becomes easier. This momentum is crucial for sustaining long-term projects.

3. **Overcoming fear**: Action is the antidote to fear. The more you act, the less intimidating your goals become. With each accomplishment, your confidence grows, reducing the power of fear over your decisions.

4. **Creating tangible results**: Ideas remain abstract until acted upon. Through action, you create tangible results that validate your efforts and inspire others to join your cause.

Doing is at the heart of legacy, and one must *do* to reach any goal. *Doing* is what makes the difference between those who say they want a legacy and those who make it materialize. The *doing, actions, steps, process, and incremental wins* all add up to the ingredients that form a memorable legacy. I encourage you to do what it takes to set realistic, achievable goals that will help maintain momentum. Large, ambitious goals can be overwhelming and sometimes too much. Break your goals down into smaller, manageable tasks that are more approachable and less daunting. Each small goal achieved builds confidence and propels you to do more to reach the next milestone.

It is important to note that legacy-building is *a marathon, not a sprint.* It's not enough to take action once or twice; sustained *doing* over time is what truly creates a lasting impact. Each day, each decision, and each step forward is a building block in the legacy you leave behind. Throughout the process, staying aligned with your core values is crucial. It's easy to get sidetracked or overwhelmed by external pressures, but remaining true to your values ensures that your actions are on point. This aligned dedication provides a sense of purpose and makes legacy creation enjoyable.

If you struggle with the *doing* part of building your legacy, know you are not alone. Many people are unsure of what to do first and what to do next. I love showing people how to break down their goals into smaller, actionable steps in my *Ignite Your Legacy* program. Then, we create a plan that outlines what needs to be done and set milestones to track their progress. In my mentoring process, I often see the desire to 'farm out' or 'offload' important responsibilities to other sources, wishing others would do the work. I can say with 100% conviction that this method will *never lead to success.* If one wants success, one must do what it takes to get there—*actions equal results.* Often, with my clients, helping them build their brands, write their books, and establish their business strategies is the first step in their legacy. I teach them how to truncate their tasks and distill the actions they must take to define their legacy. I help them build a definite message and purpose and show them how to write a best-selling book through my *Ignite Your Solo Book* program. I then work with them extensively to establish a winning brand that offers exclusive tools and techniques in my *Ignite Your Billionaire Brand Training,* setting their brand apart and offering what customers crave. I show my clients how to develop and deliver a captivating message and how to be confident on stage through my acclaimed speaking program, *Ignite Your Signature Talk.*

All of these programs require taking action and *doing* what is required to reach their desired pinnacle. What we work on primarily is how to make legacy fun, enjoyable, meaningful, and impactful. Many times, people have vision but lack the *knowing* to take the necessary steps. If you require support in executing your ideas and implementing the action necessary to formulate your legacy, reach out and book a *Discovery Call* with me, or let the team know you'd like to learn more about any of these phenomenal programs geared to inspiring action and getting results. Go to *www.igniteyou.life* to find out more, email *support@igniteyou.life*, or book a discovery call at *calendly.com/jbtime*.

It is important to acknowledge your achievement, no matter how small. Each one brings you closer to your ultimate goal and future steps. Remember, legacy is not built overnight; *it is the result of consistent and purposeful actions over time done consistently and with genuine persistence.* The best way to reach that goal is with someone at your side helping you along the way. If legacy is important in your life, let me be there to support you. I love building legacies, and I can't wait to see what we can *do* together.

As you work through the second section of the book, you will experience countless exercises that will help you *do more* and *achieve more* in this important pillar of *doing* what it takes to ignite a legacy.

Giving

Chapter 10

Prioritizing Others

The third and most difficult pillar in building a legacy is the act of GIVING before receiving. Legacy is inherently about the impact you have on others, and *giving* is at the heart of any impact you want to make. The principle of reciprocity and abundance dictates that *you must give first to receive.* Offering your time, resources, and talents selflessly creates an endless flow of *giving* that returns to you tenfold.

Giving before you receive emphasizes the importance of contributing to the well-being of others and making a positive impact on your community and beyond without compensation beforehand. A significant part of your legacy is the difference you will make in the lives of others without asking for something in return. *Giving* first encourages you to think beyond yourself and consider how you can serve and uplift those around you without always keeping score or expecting to be paid upfront.

Of course, we all deserve to be compensated for our efforts, but giving before receiving shows that you value the exchange and impact over the amount. *Giving* goes beyond dollars and cents and encourages you to offer first, whether through volunteering, mentoring, or supporting causes that align with your values—*giving* creates a generous frequency for abundance. Giving heightens the transformative power of kindness, generosity, and prosperity and empathizes these qualities to solidify a legacy. By prioritizing giving, you create an exponential effect that extends far beyond any transactions and enlivens the spirit of all those you touch.

In my work as a humanitarian, business owner, and philanthropist, I've seen the transformative power of *giving*. Whether it's emotionally supporting healing and forgiveness, mentoring emerging entrepreneurs, or funding educational initiatives, *giving* has been a cornerstone of my legacy. Offering without expecting compensation is about recognizing that *the more you give, the more you empower others* and, in turn, create a lasting source of *giving* and *receiving* for everyone to enjoy.

Giving should be a rewarding and fulfilling experience in the quest for legacy. Offering first supersedes the counting of material contributions and makes sharing knowledge, supporting others, and being there in times of need a treasured and priceless endeavor. Finding causes and motivating individuals on how they, too, can contribute meaningfully is at the heart of legacy creation. The act of *giving* bolsters a sense of community and connectedness that raises the vibration of all humanity.

The Law of Giving

When we give, we get. It is that simple. The *Law of Giving* is a fundamental principle that teaches us the profound truth that when we give, we receive in ways beyond our imagination. This universal law operates on the simple yet powerful premise that the energy and generosity we put out into the world will return to us exponentially. When we embrace the act of giving, we open ourselves up to a flow of abundance, love, and opportunities that enrich our lives in countless ways.

At the heart of the *Law of Giving* is the understanding that giving and receiving are intrinsically linked. The more we give, the more we create a positive energy flow that attracts abundance back to us. This isn't just about material wealth; it encompasses self-worth, inner fulfillment, unconditional love, and personal growth. The act of giving selflessly—whether it's our time, resources, or emotional support—creates a blossoming effect that extends far beyond the initial act, touching lives and fostering a cycle of generosity and reciprocity.

Consider the metaphor of *giving with a spoon versus giving with a shovel.* If you give only a spoonful, you will receive only a spoonful in return. However, if you give as much as possible, using the grandest means you have, the Universe responds by returning insurmountable blessings. This principle highlights the importance of giving generously and wholeheartedly. When we hold back, we limit the flow of abundance. Conversely, when we give freely and abundantly, we create space for even greater returns.

This concept is not just theoretical; it is reflected in *real-life experiences.* For example, when we offer our time to help others, we often find ourselves enriched by the connections we make and the fulfillment we feel. Similarly, when we support initiatives we care about, we experience a sense of purpose and alignment with our values. These intangible rewards often surpass the initial act of giving, filling our lives with a deeper sense of meaning and satisfaction.

The *Law of Giving* teaches us that true giving is done without expectation of return. When we give selflessly, without attachment to the outcome, we align ourselves with the natural flow of prosperity. This detachment allows us to experience the delight in giving, which is a reward in itself. The Universe recognizes this pure intention and responds by showering us with unexpected blessings and opportunities exceeding even our wildest dreams.

Embracing the *Law of Giving* requires a shift in mindset from scarcity to abundance. It involves trusting that there is enough for everyone and that we enhance our own by contributing to others' well-being. This principle challenges us to move beyond fear and distrust, encouraging us to act out of love and generosity. As we practice giving more freely, we begin to notice the many ways in which abundance flows back into our lives, often in surprising and delightful forms.

The *more we give, the more we receive,* and this exchange enriches our lives in ways that go beyond material gains and nurtures a lasting legacy. By giving abundantly and selflessly, we align ourselves with the universal flow of abundance, giving us the means to fulfill our legacy and enhance our lives. There are few more enjoyable feelings than that of reaching one's legacy markers through the act of giving.

As part of my business, I often host events, conferences, and book launches that bring people together. At all our events, the spirit of giving is at the forefront. From awarding scholarships to those in need, providing passes for family members to attend with their loved ones, and offering opportunities for volunteering and service, we ensure that giving is at the root of everything we do. We always make sure to give awards to those who have stood out and acknowledge their contributions to our community. We give prizes, gifts, and even *surprises* to those who least expect it and never ask.

We orchestrate activities that foster giving—like sharing cards, special notes, words of encouragement, or, my favorite, handing out chocolates shaped like gold coins. We ask attendees to give these chocolates to someone and tell them they are *investing* in them. This small gesture creates a true spirit of giving, support, acknowledgment, and kindness.

When our events are centered around giving, so much more unfolds. Friendships are formed, people connect, healing occurs, and a true sense of community and connection emerges from the giving nature that abounds. These moments of generosity transform our gatherings into more than just events; they become celebrations of the human spirit and the kindness giving creates.

That giving then extends beyond our events as each person returns home, blessed with the spirit of what they can give, and feels energized to carry on the sentiment. Each person leaves not merely as a participant but as a conduit. They carry the knowledge, inspiration, and unwavering commitment to action gleaned from the event. This commitment, however, is not a flickering flame destined to be extinguished. It's a tenacious ember fueled by the transformative power of giving. Since many of our attendees come from every corner of the world, we know that after an event, the law of giving exponentially spreads around the globe. It just takes one person to ignite another, and when it is done through the spirit of giving, it positively impacts many and grows exponentially.

Each act of *giving* sparked at our events has the potential to inspire countless others, creating a wave of positive change that continues to expand long after the event has ended. This global spread of *giving* is a testament to the power of connection and the enduring impact of generosity. Once ignited, the spirit of giving takes on a life of its own, weaving a tapestry of positive change across the world.

Giving at any time whether in effort, listening, understanding, showing compassion, friendships, support, or even a laugh, smile, or a hug, materializes and expands; one *giving* gesture ignites another and before you know it, everyone is *giving* the most to everyone.

The Importance of Giving in Building a Legacy

Giving is a fundamental aspect of building a legacy because it embodies the principle of contributing to something greater than oneself. Whether it's through time, resources, knowledge, or compassion, giving enhances the lives of others and creates a cumulative effect of positive change. At its core, giving is about sharing the best parts of ourselves to improve our communities and the world. This act of generosity is a powerful testament to our values and beliefs, reinforcing the impact we wish to leave behind.

Creating Meaningful Connections

One of the profound benefits of *giving* is the ability to forge meaningful connections with others. When we give, we engage with individuals and communities on a deeper level, fostering relationships built on trust, empathy, and mutual respect. These connections enrich our lives and create a network of support and collaboration that can amplify our efforts and extend our legacy's reach. By giving, we build a community of like-minded individuals who are inspired by our actions and motivated to contribute to the common good.

Amplifying Impact

Giving multiplies the impact of our efforts. By sharing our resources and knowledge, we empower others to make a difference, effectively expanding the scope of our influence. For instance, donating to educational programs not only provides immediate assistance but also equips future generations with the tools they need to succeed. Volunteering our time can inspire others to do the same, creating a culture of giving that sustains long-term change. Each act of giving sets off a chain reaction, encouraging more people to participate and contribute to the collective legacy.

Reflecting Inner Values

Our legacy is a reflection of our inner values and principles. Giving allows us to demonstrate these values in tangible ways, showcasing our commitment to the causes we care about. It sends a powerful message about what we stand for and what we hope to achieve. Whether it's supporting environmental conservation, advocating for social justice, or promoting education, our acts of giving highlight our dedication and passion. This alignment between values and actions strengthens our legacy and ensures that it forever remains authentic and meaningful.

Personal Growth and Fulfillment

Engaging in *giving* also fosters personal growth and fulfillment. It encourages us to step outside our comfort zones, develop empathy, and practice selflessness. The joy and satisfaction derived from helping others enhances our sense of purpose and well-being. This personal growth enriches our legacy, adding depth and dimension to our contributions. As we grow through giving, we become better equipped to make a lasting impact, ensuring our legacy is both impactful and rewarding.

Inspiring Future Generations

Giving sets a powerful example for future generations. It teaches the importance of generosity, compassion, and social responsibility. By embodying these principles, we inspire others, particularly younger generations, to adopt similar values and continue the cycle of giving. This ensures that our legacy is not only preserved but also perpetuated by those who follow in our footsteps. The act of giving becomes a lasting lesson, instilling a sense of duty and empowerment in the next generation.

Building a Legacy of Compassion

Ultimately, *giving* is about creating a legacy of compassion. It is about recognizing our ability to make a difference and acting on that recognition. Through giving, we leave a mark of kindness and generosity, shaping a world that values and supports one another. This compassionate legacy resonates deeply, touching the lives of countless individuals and creating a *lasting impact that transcends time.*

Giving is an indispensable element of building a legacy. It reflects our values, amplifies our impact, fosters meaningful connections, and inspires personal growth. Through *giving*, we create a legacy rich in compassion, generosity, and noticeable change. As we give, we enhance the lives of others forever impacting and influencing the trajectory of the future.

Forging a legacy is something I believe *everyone should and can do.* To help individuals reach that milestone, we have an *Ignite Your Legacy™* program that meets four times a week, sixteen times a month, to support that drive for building a legacy. No other company in the world is offering one program that addresses the trifecta of legacy creation and supports its clients in such a way. It is a monumental program designed to ensure that in twelve months, you have everything you need systematically and the tangibles you require to ensure your legacy is giving back and *giving* more. When people come to me serious about their legacy, I tell them this program is the bullet train that will get you there. If you want a proven, doable, systematized, fun-loving, and giving program to help you achieve your legacy, find out more here: *courses.igniteinstitute. life/igniteyourlegacy*.

My Commitment to Giving Back

As I embarked on my journey to build a legacy of igniting humanity, literacy became the cornerstone of my mission. As a publisher and writer, I am acutely aware of the transformative power of reading and writing. Literacy *opens doors, sparks imagination,* and equips individuals with the *tools* to communicate effectively. Books awaken the mind to new possibilities, empowering readers to dream, invent, aspire, and seek improvements on what has already been done.

I envisioned a world where children, regardless of their current living conditions or socioeconomic limitations, could access the wonders of literature. I knew that if I could help children read, I could open up a whole new world to them. Through books, they could explore new places, far-off lands, and incredible discoveries, broadening their horizons and expanding their sense of what is possible.

My dream was to build schools that would provide these children with the opportunity to learn and grow. I imagined these students as the next generation of humanitarians, leaders, visionaries, and changemakers. By enhancing their ability to read, write, and learn,

I believed I could empower them to contribute significantly to the betterment of humanity.

Literacy is not just about reading words on a page; it is about fostering a lifelong love of learning and a passion for knowledge. It is about giving children the tools they need to imagine a better future and the confidence to pursue it. *Through literacy, we can inspire them to think critically, solve problems creatively, and dream boldly.*

In building this legacy, my goal is to ignite the minds of young individuals, providing them with the skills and inspiration they need to make a difference in the world. By focusing on literacy, I hope to create positive change, where each child empowered by reading can go on to ignite the lives of others. As I became more invested in igniting literacy, I recognized the profound impact that education could have on individuals and communities. Early on, I made a conscious decision to trade royalties and dividends for the ability to use our profits to build schools in underserved areas. This commitment to education led to the creation of the *Ignite Humanity™ Foundation Fund*, a dedicated initiative to help others give in a way that supports building schools in places of need.

Building schools was just the start. I also wanted to contribute to environmental sustainability. To achieve this, I partnered with a company that makes construction blocks from recycled plastic pulled from landfills. This innovative approach not only supports the environment but also provides materials for building educational facilities. Each year, we recycle exceptional amounts of resources to raise funds and awareness, ensuring that we can give back both to the community and the planet.

My commitment to giving extends beyond financial contributions. I offer my time and efforts to support various causes, always looking for new ways to make a positive impact. Whether through volunteer work, mentoring, or cycling across the country, I believe giving back is an essential part of my mission.

I will never forget the first school we built in Lombok, Indonesia, which provided a new home for one hundred thirteen children and eleven teachers. For nearly five years, these children had been attending school in a tent due to the devastating hurricane that hit the country years earlier. The conditions were harsh, with children forced to sit on dirt floors in cramped quarters with limited supplies.

On the day we opened the school doors, the entire community gathered to welcome us. The children lined the street leading to their new school, dressed in their finest Balinese cultural attire. They sang, waved, clapped, and cheered as we walked together to the building that would become their new educational home.

As I stood surrounded by all those children, seeing their smiling faces and receiving heartfelt gratitude from the teachers, principal, and local minister of education, I turned to my husband and said, "We need to do more of this!" The feeling of giving to those people was more profound than anything I had ever experienced in a boardroom or on a stage. Hugging the children, singing, dancing, and witnessing their joy showed just how far one act of giving can go.

I know that this school will not only educate those children but also empower them to teach their parents. As the parents become better people, they will inspire those they meet and the entire village will be transformed by the gesture of giving, leaving a lasting legacy.

If you feel inspired to join me in igniting literacy, I welcome any contributions or support. Together, we can create lasting change and build a legacy of compassion and generosity. If you feel moved to contribute to our efforts, I invite you to *give* to our initiative. Your support can make a significant difference in providing education to those in need and protecting our environment. Together, we can Ignite positive change and create a better future for all. Go to *ignitehumanity.life/donate*. Every dollar buys a brick in one of our schools and becomes part of the foundation for not just a school but a life positively changed.

Chapter 11

The Power of Legacy Building

As you have learned, legacy is about the consistent, everyday actions that contribute to the well-being and upliftment of others. Whether it's through acts of kindness, advocacy, innovation, or mentorship, *every effort counts*. To form the foundations of your legacy, consider your intrinsic interests and where you intuitively feel called to *make a difference*. Identify your innate passions and think about how they can be aligned with actions that serve others. Seek out opportunities to get involved in causes that matter to you, and don't be afraid to keep going when someone gives you a "no." Remember, someone else's no is not your no, and you don't need to have all the answers or resources to forge ahead. Legacy-building is a journey, a process, and each step you take contributes to the greater impact you will eventually make.

Support yourself by taking daily actions and making a constant effort. Creating a legacy is not about waiting for everything to be perfectly aligned; it's about taking devoted actions each and every day. The following 30 daily activities are practical, actionable behaviors, tailored to help you make meaningful progress in your legacy journey.

By committing to these daily actions, you will arrive closer to your overall goal. You will cultivate a sense of purpose that will guide you in *all* areas of your life. Each day's activity builds on the previous one, creating a cumulative effect that amplifies your efforts and accelerates your growth.

Embarking on this journey requires commitment, openness, and a willingness to challenge yourself. You may encounter obstacles and setbacks along the way, but remember that each step you take, is a step toward creating your future legacy. The process of *KNOWING*, *DOING*, and *GIVING* is not always clear; therefore, it's important to be patient with yourself and stay focused on your vision of what your legacy means to you.

No one but you defines your legacy. That means you are the only one who can do the work and master the results. The 30 ways suggested here are insightful ways for you to challenge old ideals while formulating new defining cornerstones for your ideal legacy. Trial and error are part of the process as much as achievement and success—analyze all your actions and observe how each suggestion feels *within* your heart. Alignment is key to making sure your legacy is sustainable and warrants your full commitment.

Defining Your Legacy

Now is your opportunity to embark on the path of legacy-building. Take this journey with the understanding that building a legacy is achievable for you. It starts with small, deliberate actions that reflect your values and aspirations. Let the *Three Pillars* guide you, making the path to your legacy both attainable and rewarding. The time to start building your legacy is now, as you begin with focused, daily actions that gradually increase to create a significant impact.

Every day, commit to doing the prompt designed to develop different facets of your legacy. Whether you're an author, coach, entrepreneur, educator, or someone devoted to personal growth, spirituality, or positive consciousness—these steps will equip you with the tools and inspiration to create a lasting and meaningful legacy.

My aim has always been to make the journey of igniting a legacy enjoyable, straightforward, and filled with practical steps to achieve it. By working through these suggestions, you can expedite the process of creating a legacy into manageable and engaging steps. Legacy-building doesn't need to be overwhelming; it can be an enriching adventure filled with moments of joy, personal growth, and meaningful connections.

Using this book, embark on a 30-day journey where each day brings you closer to building the legacy you dream of. This journey is not about grand gestures but the meaningful steps that accumulate over time to create impact. Each day, you will explore different aspects of the *Three Pillars*, discovering practical and enjoyable ways to integrate them into your life.

Over the next 30 days, each activity will deepen your self-awareness, inspire you to take purposeful action, and encourage you to give in ways that multiply. You'll find that legacy-building can be an endearing and enlightening process, one that fills your life with a sense of purpose and fulfillment. As you progress, you'll experience moments of growth and transformation, realizing that every step you take contributes to the greater good.

By the end of this journey, you will have not only laid the foundation for your legacy, but also cultivated habits and ideas that will continue to support you long after the 30 days are over. You'll see how each action, amidst all the pillars, is a vital part of the larger framework of your legacy. This journey *will* transform your perspective, showing you that building a legacy is not a distant dream but a daily practice filled with potential and possibility.

By doing these 30 activities, you will achieve a greater connection to your legacy and contribute positively and effectively to the world around you. Each one represents a crucial aspect of creating a meaningful and lasting impact. By dedicating time and effort to all these principles, you will cultivate a winning approach to defining your legacy and making a societal contribution that you will be forever proud of.

Knowing
Days 1-6

Chapter 12

Know Your Legacy

*O*ver the next 6 days, you will embark on a series of prompts designed to grow the *Pillar of Knowing*. This foundational pillar is all about deepening your self-awareness, understanding of your core values, *and* clarifying your purpose. By dedicating time each day to these exercises, you will begin to uncover the essence of who you are and what drives you, setting the stage for a meaningful and impactful legacy.

Each day, you will be guided through a focused activity encouraging introspection and personal growth. These prompts are designed to be both thought-provoking and actionable, helping you to gradually build a strong sense of inner knowing. As you engage with each exercise, take your time to reflect deeply and honestly. The insights you gain will be invaluable as you move forward in creating your legacy.

Establishing a Knowing that Guides Your Legacy

At the heart of *knowing are* the core concepts of self-awareness and understanding along with the principles of frequency and mindset.

Imagine a world where every thought, action, and decision resonates with a powerful frequency, shaping the reality around us. *Knowing* starts with frequency and realizing that everything in our Universe vibrates within its own *unique* energy. From the tiniest atoms to the grandest galaxies, an invisible symphony of vibrations is constantly playing out. *And, the most incredible part?* We have the power to tune into and harness these frequencies to shape our lives. This isn't just new-age mysticism—it's science! Our thoughts and emotions emit specific frequencies, impacting our personal experiences and the people and opportunities that come into our lives.

Mindset is the lens through which we view the world and it shapes all that we do. Our mindset determines our outlook, beliefs, and attitudes toward our actions. It's the silent force that either propels us upwards or holds us back. As we explore the *knowing* around our frequency and mindset, we'll uncover their profound impact on our daily lives and how, by unharnessing them, we can unlock extraordinary possibilities that help us build our legacy.

I often say, "The frequency you draw from determines the actions you take, which produces the impact you will make." *What frequency are you using to build your legacy? What knowing is in your spirit that guides your attitude and beliefs?* How we think of things and how we react directly collate with what we produce. Working on the mind, knowing, and internal beliefs is the place to start when it comes to shaping one's legacy.

Set a specific time each day to read each prompt and be consistent in working thoroughly and completing them with patience, perseverance, and caring grace. How we do one thing is how we do everything, so how you approach each prompt will determine the results you receive in return.

Understanding Frequency and Mindset

Your mindset is the foundation upon which all your actions are built. The frequency you operate on—your thoughts, emotions, and attitudes—directly influences the quality of your life and the im`pact you make.

Your mindset is the foundation upon which all your actions are built. The frequency you operate on—your thoughts, emotions, and attitudes—directly influences the quality of your life and the impact you make. When your thoughts are positive and aligned with your goals, you are more likely to take actions that lead to success. Conversely, negative thoughts can hinder your progress and keep you stuck in unproductive patterns.

Understanding your frequency involves recognizing the energy you emit and how it affects your life. This energy can be high or low, positive or negative. High-frequency thoughts are uplifting, optimistic, and empowering. They inspire you to move forward, take risks, and believe in your potential. Low-frequency thoughts, on the other hand, are often negative, fearful, and limiting. They hold you back and create obstacles to your success.

Task: Spend ten minutes meditating on positive affirmations that align with your goals. Begin by finding a quiet space where you won't be disturbed. Sit comfortably and close your eyes. Take a few deep breaths to center yourself. Then, repeat positive affirmations that resonate with you. For instance, "I am capable of achieving my goals," "I am worthy of success," and "I attract positive energy and opportunities." Feel the truth of these statements as you say them. This practice helps you tune into a higher frequency, setting the stage for transformative actions.

Action Step: Reflect on your current mindset and identify areas for positive frequency tuning. Write down any negative thoughts or beliefs that come to mind. Challenge these thoughts by asking yourself if they are really true. Replace them with positive affirmations that support your goals. Commit to repeating these affirmations daily, especially when you notice negative thoughts creeping in.

Dip into the Frequency of Ignite

The word I.G.N.I.T.E. encapsulates the essential elements of success: **Inspire, Give, Nurture, Improve, Transform**, *and* **Empower**. *Integrating these elements into your daily life creates a positive feedback loop that propels you towards your goals.*

The IGNITE frequency is more than just a set of words; it's a mindset and a way of life that can profoundly impact your journey toward success. Each element of the IGNITE frequency plays a crucial role in shaping your actions and outcomes. Ignite symbolizes the ability to light the way and draw from a source that epitomizes the essence of sparking new thoughts and burning strong. It is important to pull from a philosophy that activates and inspires ignition. Use the essence of IGNITE to propel you.

- **Inspire**: Inspiration is the spark that ignites creativity and motivation. It drives you to think beyond your current circumstances and envision a brighter future.

- **Give**: Giving is about contributing your time, energy, and resources to others. It creates a sense of purpose and fulfillment.

- **Nurture**: Nurturing involves caring for yourself and others, fostering growth and development.

- **Improve**: Continuous improvement is essential for progress. It's about striving to be better today than you were yesterday.

- **Transform**: Transformation is the process of profound change. It involves letting go of old patterns and embracing new ways of being.

- **Empower**: Empowerment is about gaining the confidence and strength to take control of your life and help others do the same.

Task: Write down one way you can incorporate each element of the IGNITE frequency into your daily routine. For example, *inspire* yourself by reading motivational books, *give* by helping a colleague, *nurture* your growth through continuous learning, *improve* a skill each day, *transform* your habits, and *empower* others through your generous actions.

Action Step: Create a daily plan that includes activities for each IGNITE element. For example:

Inspire: Read a chapter from a motivational book.

Give: Offer to help a colleague with their project.

Nurture: Spend thirty minutes practicing self-care.

Improve: Learn a new skill or technique.

Transform: Identify and change one limiting habit.

Empower: Share your knowledge or skills with someone who can benefit.

Inspiring Yourself and Others

Inspiration is a driving force that fuels creativity and perseverance. When you are inspired, you are more likely to take bold actions and overcome obstacles.

Inspiration is the spark that Ignites your inner fire. It fuels your passion, creativity, and perseverance. When inspired, you are more likely to take bold actions, overcome obstacles, and achieve your goals. Inspiration can come from various sources, such as books, people, nature, or personal experiences.

To inspire yourself, start by identifying what excites and motivates you. *What are your passions and interests? What dreams do you want to achieve?* Surround yourself with positive influences that uplift and encourage you. This could be motivational books, inspiring people, or uplifting environments.

Inspiring others involves sharing your passion and positivity. When you inspire others, you create a ripple effect that spreads positive energy and motivation. Your actions and words can have a profound impact on those around you, encouraging them to pursue their own dreams and goals.

Task: Write down three ways to inspire yourself and others. You could start by sharing an inspiring story or quote on social media, creating a vision board that visualizes your goals, and setting a new personal challenge that excites you. For instance, if you've overcome a significant challenge in your life, share your story to motivate others facing similar obstacles. Create a motivation poster with images and quotes representing your goals and aspirations. Set a personal challenge, like running a marathon or writing a book, and document your journey to inspire others.

Action Step: Choose one of the three ways you identified and take action today. For example, if you share an inspiring story, write a post on social media or your blog detailing your experience and the lessons you learned. If you create a vision board, gather images, quotes, and other materials that resonate with your goals and start assembling them. If you decide to set a personal challenge, outline the steps you need to take and start working toward it. Put it into motion and share your intention with others to solidify your goal.

The Power of Giving

Giving is a fundamental principle that enriches both the giver and the receiver. When you give, you open yourself up to receiving more in return.

Giving is a powerful principle that can transform your life and the lives of others. It's not just about giving material things; it's about giving your time, energy, and love. When you give, you create a sense of connection and community. You also open yourself up to receiving more in return, as giving creates a positive energy flow.

Giving can take many forms, from helping a friend in need to volunteering your time for a cause you care about. It's about being generous with your resources, whether it's your time, skills, or money.

When you give selflessly, you create a massive effect of positivity that can transform many lives.

Task: Plan a small act of giving today. This could be donating to a local charity, helping a colleague with a project, or spending time volunteering. For instance, you could donate clothes or food to a local shelter, offer your expertise to help a colleague with a challenging task, or volunteer at a community center or animal shelter. These acts of generosity benefit others and enrich your life, fostering a sense of fulfillment and abundance.

Action Step: Choose one of the small acts of giving you identified and take action today. For example, if you decide to donate to a local charity, gather items you no longer need and take them to the donation center. If you choose to help a colleague, offer your assistance and make time in your schedule to support them. If you decide to volunteer, find an opportunity that fits your interests and availability and sign up to help.

Nurturing Your Potential

To reach your full potential, it is crucial to nurture your talents and passions. This involves dedicating time and resources to personal growth and self-care.

Nurturing your potential involves recognizing and cultivating your talents, passions, and abilities. It's about dedicating time and resources to personal growth and self-care. When you nurture your potential, you create the conditions for your talents and passions to flourish.

Self-care is a critical component of nurturing your potential. It involves taking care of your physical, emotional, and mental well-being. This includes regular exercise, healthy eating, sufficient rest, and engaging in activities that bring you joy and relaxation. Self-care helps you recharge and maintain the energy and focus needed to pursue your goals.

Personal growth involves continuous learning and development. It's about seeking out opportunities to learn new skills, gain knowledge, and expand your horizons. This could be through formal education, professional development, or personal experiences. By prioritizing personal growth, you enhance your ability to contribute meaningfully to your mission.

Task: Create a self-nurturing plan that includes activities you love, such as pursuing a hobby, enrolling in an online course, or setting aside time for relaxation and reflection. For instance, if you enjoy painting, set aside time each week to work on your art. If you're interested in a specific topic, enroll in an online course to deepen your knowledge. Make time for relaxation and reflection by scheduling regular breaks and engaging in activities like meditation or journaling.

Action Step: Implement your self-nurturing plan right now. Choose one self-care activity and take action. For example, if you decide to pursue a hobby, gather the materials you need and set aside dedicated time to work on it. If you choose to enroll in an online course, research available options and sign up for one that interests you. If you decide to set aside time for relaxation and reflection, create a schedule that includes regular breaks and self-care activities. Then, add nurturing additions to fill your senses with calming music, fresh scents, tantalizing tastes, and a soothing experience.

Day 6: Improving Continuously

Continuous improvement is a pathway to long-term success. Embrace the mindset that there is always room for growth and learning.

Continuous improvement is the process of constantly seeking ways to enhance your skills, knowledge, and performance. Gaining skills to support your growth is about embracing the mindset that there is *always* room for expansion and learning. When you commit to continuous improvement, you make steady progress toward your goals and set a powerful example for others.

Improvement can take many forms, from developing new skills to refining existing ones. It's about being proactive in identifying areas where you can improve and taking action to address them. This might involve seeking feedback from others, setting specific learning goals, or experimenting with new approaches.

The key to continuous improvement is a growth mindset. This is the belief that your abilities and intelligence can be developed through dedication and hard work. A growth mindset fosters a love of learning and resilience in the face of challenges. It encourages you to view setbacks as opportunities for growth and to persist in the pursuit of your goals.

Task: Identify one area where you can improve and take a step toward it. This could involve reading a book on a skill you want to develop, practicing a new technique, or seeking feedback from a mentor. For instance, if you want to improve your public speaking skills, read a book on effective communication techniques, practice speaking in front of a mirror, or seek feedback from a mentor who is an experienced speaker.

Action Step: Take action to improve in the area you identified. For example, if you decide to read a book on a skill, choose a book and start reading a chapter today. If you choose to practice a new technique, set aside time to practice and refine your skills. If you decide to seek feedback from a mentor, reach out to them and schedule a time to discuss your progress and areas for improvement.

Chapter 13

Expand Your Knowingness

Well done on completing the first pillar of Igniting your legacy: *knowing*. You have worked hard to uncover and reveal new and informative parts of yourself that will add to the framework of your legacy. *Knowing* is an ongoing process, and like an onion with many layers, continues to unfurl new ideas and opportunities. Knowing is an ever-changing process with no end point, so trust that as your legacy unfolds it will do so as you learn more, expand your thinking, and awaken your consciousness.

If you enjoyed this part of the process, you can always continue digging deeper by attending our weekly classes on *Ignite Your Breakthrough*, a transformative, ongoing mastermind designed to help you overcome preconditions and limiting beliefs, aligning you more deeply with your inner knowing and broadening your beliefs. We are seldom shown how to trust our intuition or cultivate a strong connection with our inner self. This class is dedicated to reversing that trend, empowering you to tap into the greatest source of wisdom and guidance available: *your own inner knowing and deep convictions.*

Each week, we gather to explore powerful mindset tools and strategies that enable you to break free from the constraints that have held you back. Our sessions are designed to be both practical and inspirational, providing you with tangible techniques to connect with your inner voice and trust its guidance. By doing so, you become more aligned with your true self and are better equipped to pursue your legacy with clarity and confidence.

Ignite Your Breakthrough is more than just training; *it's a supportive community where you can share your understanding with like-minded individuals.* Together, we dive into simple yet profound strategies that help you develop a stronger connection to your inner self. Each session is tailored to help you cultivate a deeper sense of trust and alignment with your core beliefs. As you build on these strategies, you will find yourself more attuned to your inner calling, ready to overcome any barriers, and poised to make a lasting impact in the world.

I'll admit that building a legacy is a mental process, and working on my thoughts, patterns, and beliefs was imperative if I wanted to succeed. I took many classes, read many books, and asked as many questions as possible to prepare myself emotionally, spiritually, and mentally for the process. Legacy building is not meant to be done alone, and the more people I found to coach, mentor, and guide me, the faster I achieved my goals and the sooner my legacy was being formulated.

Building your legacy requires being open-minded, constantly learning, and embracing change. Effective communication skills are essential for building trust, rapport, and relaying information. A successful legacy maker must be a good listener, pay close attention to their goals, and develop personalized action plans to reach their desired breakthrough.

If you want to *Ignite Your Breakthrough* and take the first step toward a more empowered and aligned life, sign up now and join our weekly membership.

Chapter 14

The Power of Daily Doing

The power of daily actions lies in one's ability to create significant change through consistent effort. While big gestures and major accomplishments are often celebrated, it is the small, deliberate steps taken every day that truly shape our lives and build our legacies. By committing to daily actions, you establish a routine that fosters continuous progress and development. Though seemingly minor, these actions accumulate over time to produce the results you seek. This consistent approach ensures that you are always moving forward, even if the steps are not noticeable initially.

Daily actions provide a sense of structure and purpose. When you set clear, actionable daily goals, you create a roadmap that guides your journey. This structure not only helps you stay focused and organized but also provides a sense of accomplishment as you check off each task. The discipline of daily actions builds momentum, making it easier to maintain motivation and drive. Each completed task serves as a beacon, bringing you closer to your larger objectives and reinforcing the habit of productivity.

Daily actions allow for continuous learning and improvement. By engaging in regular practice and reflection, you gain insights into what works and what doesn't. This iterative process enables you to refine your approach, account for new skills, and adapt to changing circumstances. The incremental progress made through daily actions helps you build a strong foundation of knowledge and experience. Over time, these gradual improvements lead to significant growth, enhancing your ability to achieve more goals.

The impact of daily actions influences the people and environments around you. Consistent efforts in kindness, collaboration, and community involvement can create a positive chain reaction. When others see your commitment to daily actions, they are often inspired to follow suit, amplifying the overall impact. This collective effort can drive substantial change in communities and organizations on a global scale. Daily actions not only contribute to your legacy but also help *shape a better world for all to enjoy.*

The power of daily actions lies in their simplicity and accessibility. By focusing on what you can do each day, you empower yourself to take control of your destiny and create a meaningful legacy. The cumulative effect of these actions builds a lasting impact that reflects your values and aspirations. Embrace the power of daily actions and witness how these small steps can lead to extraordinary achievements and a fulfilling life.

The next 18 days will be the bulk of your physical efforts. Each day will consist of something tangible you can do to move the needle forward in your legacy pursuits. There are a plethora of actions, steps, and tasks you can take that will strengthen your *doing* muscles and increase your results. As you do each one, consider how it will add to your legacy and how you can use what you are learning to bring you that much closer to the legacy you dream of.

Doing
Days 7-20

Chapter 15

Doing Creates Legacy

Setting big, audacious goals is exhilarating and can ignite a fire within us to achieve greatness. However, the path to reaching these monumental aspirations can often seem daunting and overwhelming. This is where the art of breaking down big goals comes into play. By dissecting your grand vision into smaller, manageable milestones, you make the process less intimidating and *increase your chances of success.* Imagine a colossal mountain standing before you, its peak shrouded in mist and mystery. Your goal is to conquer this mountain, but the sheer magnitude of the task leaves you feeling uncertain. Now, instead of staring at the summit with trepidation, picture yourself taking each step methodically, focusing on the immediate terrain rather than the distant peak. This approach transforms an intimidating feat into a series of achievable steps.

Breaking down big goals allows you to establish a clear roadmap for your journey. Each sub-goal acts as a stepping stone, leading you closer to the ultimate prize. The sense of accomplishment derived from conquering these smaller objectives serves as a powerful motivator, propelling you forward with renewed vigor and esteem. In addition to mitigating feelings of being overwhelmed, breaking down big goals also provides the opportunity for course correction and adaptation. As you accomplish each mini-milestone, you gain valuable insights and feedback that can be used to refine your approach and ensure you stay aligned with your final objective.

Consider this analogy: *building a magnificent mansion starts with laying the foundation, erecting the framework, and gradually adding intricate details.* Similarly, breaking down big goals involves constructing a sturdy base through incremental progress, bolstering it with each small victory, and eventually witnessing your masterwork come to fruition. Enjoy the process of deconstructing your ambitious goals into manageable segments, and marvel at how it empowers you to strive toward excellence. The journey from aspiration to realization becomes an adventure filled with triumphs, learning experiences, and the unyielding spirit of perseverance.

Focus on taking action toward your legacy, breaking down big goals into micro goals, and *doing* what it takes to establish winning results.

Defining Your Mission

A clear, measurable mission provides direction and purpose. It acts as a compass, guiding your decisions and actions.

Defining your mission is a crucial step in achieving your legacy. Your mission statement clearly and concisely declares your purpose and objectives. It provides direction and serves as a compass, guiding your decisions and actions. A well-defined mission helps you stay focused and motivated, even in the face of challenges.

Your mission statement should reflect your core values and objectives. It should answer the questions: *What do you want to achieve? Why is it important? How will you achieve it?* A clear mission statement guides your actions and communicates your purpose to others, inspiring them to support your efforts.

Task: Write down your mission statement, reflecting your core values and objectives. For instance, if you are an entrepreneur, your mission statement might be: "To create innovative products that improve the lives of our customers and contribute to a sustainable future." If you are a life coach, your mission statement might be: "To empower individuals to achieve their full potential through personalized coaching and support." A mission statement gives you a clear directive as to where you are headed and where you want to reach. It helps you hit your target and stay on point.

Action Step: Craft your mission statement today. Reflect on your core values and objectives, and write a concise statement that encapsulates your purpose and goals for your legacy. Share your mission statement with someone you trust and ask for their feedback. Refine your statement based on their input, and commit to using it as a guide for your decisions and actions.

Breaking Down Big Goals

Big goals can often feel overwhelming, making it easy to procrastinate. The key to overcoming this is breaking them down into manageable micro goals.

Big goals can often feel overwhelming, making it easy to procrastinate or give up. The key to overcoming this is breaking them down into manageable micro goals. Micro goals are truncated, actionable steps that move you closer to your larger objective. By tackling one small task at a time, you make consistent progress at a steady gate.

Breaking down big goals involves identifying the individual tasks and milestones needed to achieve your overall objective. This might involve creating a detailed action plan that outlines each step and its associated timeline. By focusing on one micro goal at a time, you build momentum and stay motivated.

Task: If your goal is to write a book, break it down into steps like researching, outlining, writing chapters, and editing. For instance, start with the research phase by identifying the topics you need to explore and gathering relevant resources. Next, outline the structure of your book, including the main sections and chapters. Then, set specific goals for writing each chapter, and finally, plan time for editing and revising your manuscript. If your goal is to build a brand, invent a product, open a non-profit, or design a solution to an ongoing problem, identify each step in the process and break it down into doable points.

Action Step: Identify your big goal and break it down into smaller, actionable micro goals. Create a detailed action plan that outlines each step and its associated timeline. For example:

- **Step 1:** Research and gather resources.

- **Step 2:** Outline the established needs.

- **Steps 3-8:** Identify key markers and success points.

- **Steps 9-10:** Gather support, revenue, or tools.

Commit to focusing on one micro goal at a time, and celebrate your progress as you complete each step.

Making a 1% Improvement Daily

The compound effect of small, consistent improvements is powerful. By focusing on making a 1% improvement each day, you create significant progress over time.

The concept of making a 1% improvement daily is based on the idea that small, consistent changes can lead to significant progress over time. This principle, often referred to as the compound effect, highlights how incremental improvements can accumulate to create substantial results.

By focusing on making a 1% improvement each day, you build positive habits and continuously move towards your goals. These small changes might seem insignificant on their own, but over time, they compound to create meaningful progress. The key is to be consistent and persistent, making small improvements a part of your daily routine.

Task: Identify one small improvement you can implement today. This could be enhancing your workspace organization, learning a new productivity hack, or refining a daily habit. For instance, you might decide to organize your workspace by decluttering and setting up a more efficient system. Alternatively, you could learn a new productivity technique, app, or skill to help you manage your time more effectively. Or, you might refine a daily habit, such as balancing your P&L (profit and loss), or creating a costing forecast.

Action Step: Choose one small improvement and take action today. For example, decide to enhance your workspace organization, spend time decluttering your desk, organizing your files, and setting up a system that works for you. Choose to learn a new productivity hack, research the Pomodoro Technique, and implement it in your daily routine. Commit to refining a daily habit, like setting a practice gratitude each morning, or breathing techniques to feel motivated.

Establishing Winning Behaviors

Your behaviors influence your success. Establishing winning behaviors involves adopting habits that support your goals.

Winning behaviors are the habits and actions that support your goals and contribute to your success. These behaviors are often the result of intentional effort and discipline. By identifying and adopting winning behaviors, you create a strong foundation for achieving your objectives.

Establishing winning behaviors involves understanding the actions and habits that lead to success in your specific field or area of interest. This might include behaviors such as setting investment goals, implementing forgiveness practices, staying organized, being proactive, or integrating restful sleep. By consistently practicing helpful behaviors, you increase your chances of success and reduce any stress.

Task: Start by incorporating a morning routine that sets a positive tone for the day. This could include exercise, journaling, or planning your day. For instance, you might begin your day with a 30-minute workout to boost your energy levels. Follow this with a journaling session where you reflect on your goals and intentions for the day. Finally, spend a few minutes planning your day, prioritizing tasks, and setting clear goals.

Action Step: Establish a morning routine that includes winning behaviors. Start by choosing activities that align with your goals and set a positive tone for the day. For example:

- **Exercise:** Choose a workout routine that suits your fitness level and preferences.

- **Journaling:** Reflect on your goals, intentions, and any insights or lessons learned.

- **Planning:** Systemize your tasks, map out clear goals, and create a cadence for the day.

Commit to practicing your morning routine consistently, and adjust it as needed to ensure it continues to support your goals.

Producing Deliverables

Delivering what customers want and solving their problems is crucial for success. List the deliverables you can provide to your audience.

Producing deliverables involves creating products, services, or content that meet the needs and desires of your audience. It's about understanding what your customers want and providing solutions to their problems. *By focusing on delivering value, you build trust and credibility with your audience, which is essential for long-term success.*

To produce effective deliverables, start by identifying the needs and preferences of your audience. This might involve conducting market research, gathering feedback, or analyzing trends. Once you have a clear understanding of what your audience wants, you can develop products, services, or content that address their needs and provide real value.

Task: List the deliverables you can provide to your audience. This might include creating a free ebook, developing a webinar, or launching a new service. For instance, if you are a professional, you might create a free ebook that provides valuable insights and tips related to your expertise. If you are a fitness coach, you might develop a webinar that addresses common challenges faced by your clients. If you are a business owner, you might launch a new service that solves a specific problem for your customers.

Action Step: Choose one deliverable and take action to produce it. For example, decide to create a free ebook, outline the content you want to include, write the chapters, and design the layout. choose to develop a webinar, plan the topics you want to cover, create a presentation, and schedule a time to deliver it. Decide to launch a new service, outline the features and benefits, develop a marketing plan, and start promoting it to your audience.

Creating Core Beliefs

Your core beliefs shape your actions and decisions. Identify and write down your core beliefs, reflecting on how they guide your behavior.

Core beliefs are the fundamental principles and values that guide your actions and decisions. They shape your worldview and influence how you respond to various situations. Understanding and aligning with your core beliefs is essential for achieving your goals and living a fulfilling life.

To identify your core beliefs, reflect on what is most important to you. Consider your values, principles, and the guiding forces in your life. Your core beliefs should resonate with your inner self and provide a strong foundation for your actions and decisions.

Task: Identify and write down your core beliefs, reflecting on how they guide your behavior. For instance, if you value integrity, you might write: "I believe in being honest and transparent in all my interactions." If you value growth, you might write: "I believe in continuously learning and improving myself." If you value compassion, you might write: "I believe in treating others with kindness and empathy."

Action Step: Reflect on your core beliefs and write them down. Consider how these beliefs guide your actions and decisions. For example:

- **Integrity:** Reflect on how being honest and transparent has positively impacted your life and relationships.

- **Growth:** Consider the steps you take to continuously learn and improve, and how this has contributed to your success.

- **Compassion:** Think about the ways you demonstrate kindness and empathy, and how this has strengthened your connections with others.

Revisit your core beliefs regularly and ensure that your actions align with them. This alignment will help you stay true to yourself and achieve your goals in a meaningful way.

Establishing a Baseline

Knowing where you stand is essential for measuring progress. Establish a baseline for your goals by measuring current performance metrics.

Establishing a baseline is crucial for tracking your progress and measuring success. A baseline provides a reference point that allows you to assess your current performance and identify areas for improvement. It involves measuring key metrics related to your goals and documenting them as a starting point.

To establish a baseline, identify the key performance indicators (KPIs) that are relevant to your goals. These might include metrics such as sales numbers, audience engagement, productivity levels, or personal milestones. By documenting your current performance, you create a clear picture of where you stand and what needs to be improved.

Task: Measure current performance metrics, such as sales numbers, audience engagement, or personal milestones. For instance, if you are a solopreneur, you might measure your monthly sales figures, website traffic, and customer satisfaction levels. If you are a successful coach, you might track the number of clients you have, the success rate of your coaching programs, and client feedback. If you are focused on personal development, you might track milestones such as completing courses, achieving fitness goals, or maintaining a daily routine.

- **Action Step:** Establish a baseline for your goals by measuring and documenting your current performance metrics. For example:

- **Sales numbers:** Record your monthly sales figures and identify trends.

- **Audience engagement:** Track metrics such as website traffic, social media engagement, and email open rates.

- **Personal milestones:** Document your achievements in areas such as education, fitness, or personal growth.

Use this baseline to set specific, measurable goals and track your progress over time. Regularly review your performance metrics and adjust your strategies as needed to ensure continuous improvement.

Exploring the Essence of You

Delve into your true essence and passions to uncover what truly drives you. Reflect on and document your core passions, considering both personal and professional aspects.

Exploring the essence of you involves understanding your true self and what drives you. It's about delving into your core passions, interests, and motivations. When you connect with your true essence, you gain clarity on what brings you joy and fulfillment, both personally and professionally.

To explore the essence of you, start by reflecting on your interests and passions. What activities make you feel alive and energized? What are you naturally drawn to? Consider both personal and professional aspects, as they often overlap and influence each other.

Understanding your true essence helps you align your actions with what genuinely excites and motivates you. This alignment leads to more fulfilling and impactful outcomes, as you are driven by a deep sense of purpose and passion.

Task: Reflect on and document your core passions, considering both personal and professional aspects. For instance, if you are passionate about helping others, you might document experiences where you felt most fulfilled while supporting someone. If you love creativity, you might reflect on moments when you were deeply engaged in artistic activities. If you have a strong interest in personal development, you might consider times when you were actively learning and growing.

Action Step: Write about your core passions and how they influence your actions and decisions. For example:

- **Helping others:** Reflect on how your passion for helping others has guided your career choices and personal interactions.

- **Creativity:** Consider how your love for creativity has influenced your projects and hobbies.

- **Personal development:** Think about the ways your interest in personal growth has shaped your learning experiences and achievements.

Use this reflection to identify activities and goals that align with your true essence. Commit to pursuing these passions and integrating them into your daily life.

Reevaluating Your Beliefs

Periodic reevaluation of your beliefs ensures that they remain aligned with your goals. Challenge any limiting beliefs and replace them with empowering ones.

Reevaluating your beliefs involves regularly assessing your core principles and values to ensure they remain aligned with your goals. This process helps you stay flexible and open to new possibilities, fostering continuous growth and adaptation. Beliefs that may have served you in the past might need to be updated or replaced as you evolve and pursue new goals.

Limiting beliefs are thoughts or convictions that hold you back and prevent you from reaching your full potential. *These beliefs often stem from past experiences, societal conditioning, or self-doubt.* Challenging and replacing these limiting beliefs with empowering ones is crucial for personal and professional growth.

Empowering beliefs are positive, constructive thoughts that support your goals and aspirations. They inspire confidence, resilience, and a proactive mindset. By regularly reevaluating your beliefs, you ensure that your mindset remains conducive to success and fulfillment.

Task: Identify and challenge any limiting beliefs that might be holding you back. For instance, if you believe that you are not good enough to achieve your goals, challenge this belief by asking yourself if it is really true. Look for evidence that contradicts this belief, such as past achievements and positive feedback from others. Replace the limiting belief with an empowering one, such as "I am capable of achieving my goals and deserving of success."

Action Step: Reflect on your current beliefs and identify any that might be limiting your potential. Write down these limiting beliefs and challenge them by questioning their validity and looking for evidence that disproves them. Replace each limiting belief with an empowering belief that supports your goals. For example:

- **Limiting Belief:** "I am not good enough."

- **Empowering Belief:** "I am capable and deserving of success."

Commit to practicing these empowering beliefs daily, especially when you notice negative thoughts creeping in. Regularly reevaluate your beliefs to ensure they remain aligned with your evolving goals.

Getting Centered

Centering yourself is crucial for maintaining focus on your mission. Practice a centering exercise, such as mindfulness meditation, deep breathing exercises, or a grounding activity.

Getting centered involves grounding yourself in the present moment and maintaining a clear focus on your mission. It's about creating a sense of calm and balance that allows you to navigate challenges with clarity and resilience. Centering practices help you stay focused, reduce stress, and enhance your overall well-being.

Mindfulness meditation is a powerful centering practice that involves paying attention to the present moment without judgment. It helps you cultivate awareness and focus, allowing you to stay centered even in the midst of chaos. Deep breathing exercises are another effective centering technique that can calm the mind and reduce stress. Grounding activities, such as spending time in nature or practicing yoga, can also help you stay centered and connected to your mission.

Task: Practice a centering exercise, such as mindfulness meditation, deep breathing exercises, or a grounding activity. For instance, you might start your day with a 10-minute mindfulness meditation session. Find a quiet space, sit comfortably, and focus on your breath. Notice the sensation of the breath entering and leaving your body. If your mind wanders, gently bring your focus back to your breath. Alternatively, you could practice deep breathing exercises by inhaling deeply through your nose, holding your breath for a few seconds, and exhaling slowly through your mouth. Another option is to engage in a grounding activity, such as taking a walk in nature or practicing yoga.

Action Step: Choose a centering exercise and incorporate it into your daily routine. For example:

- **Mindfulness meditation:** Set aside 10 minutes each morning to practice mindfulness meditation.

- **Deep breathing exercises:** Take a few minutes during the day to practice deep breathing, especially during stressful moments.

- **Grounding activity:** Schedule regular time for a grounding activity, such as spending time in nature or practicing yoga.

Commit to practicing your chosen centering exercise consistently, and notice how it helps you stay focused and balanced.

Want to Be Known For

Clarity on the legacy you want to leave is vital for purposeful action. Define how you want to be remembered, considering the impact you want to make and the values you want to embody.

Deciding what you want to be known for involves reflecting on the legacy you want to leave behind. It's about understanding the impact you want to make and the values you want to embody. This clarity helps you align your actions with your long-term vision and ensures that your efforts contribute to a meaningful legacy.

To define what you want to be known for, consider your core values, principles, and the ideology you want to benefit the world. Reflect on how you want to be remembered by your family, friends, colleagues, and community. Think about the qualities and achievements that you want to be associated with your name.

Having a clear vision of your desired legacy provides direction and motivation. It helps you stay focused on what truly matters and guides your decisions and actions. When you know what you want to be known for, you are more likely to take purposeful actions that align with your long-term goals.

Task: Define how you want to be remembered, considering the impact you want to make and the values you want to embody. For instance, if you value integrity and compassion, you might want to be remembered as someone who always acted with honesty and kindness. If you are passionate about education, you might want to be known for your contributions to improving access to quality education. If you aspire to be a leader in your field, you might want to be remembered for your innovative ideas and positive influence.

Action Step: Write a personal vision statement that outlines your desired legacy. Reflect on your core values, passions, and the impact you want to make. For example:

- "I want to be remembered as a compassionate leader who always acted with integrity and inspired others to achieve their full potential."

- "I want to be known for my contributions to improving access to quality education and empowering individuals through knowledge."

- "I aspire to leave a legacy of innovation and positive influence in my field, making a meaningful impact on the lives of others."

Commit to aligning your actions with your vision statement and regularly revisit it to ensure you stay focused on your desired legacy.

Choosing Your Well

Deciding what resources and strengths you will draw from is essential for sustained success. Identify your primary sources of inspiration and strength.

Choosing your well involves identifying the resources, strengths, and sources of inspiration that you will draw from to achieve your goals. It's about understanding what fuels your motivation and sustains your efforts. By tapping into these sources, you ensure that you have the support and energy needed for sustained success.

To choose your well, reflect on the people, practices, and environments that inspire and empower you. This might include mentors, books, practices, exercises, or supportive communities. Understanding your sources of inspiration and strength helps you stay motivated and resilient, even in the face of challenges.

Your well can also include your inherent strengths and talents. Recognizing and leveraging these strengths allows you to maximize your potential and achieve your goals more effectively. By drawing from your well, you ensure that you have a solid foundation to support your journey.

Task: Identify your primary sources of inspiration and strength. For instance, you might find inspiration from a mentor who has achieved what you aspire to accomplish. You might draw strength from practices such as daily affirmations, interval exercise, or listening to motivational audiobooks. You might also find support and encouragement from a community of like-minded individuals who share your goals and values.

Action Step: Make a list of your primary sources of inspiration and strength. For example:

- **Mentors**: Identify individuals who inspire you and can offer guidance and support.

- **Practices:** List daily practices that help you stay focused and energized.

- **Community:** Identify supportive communities or networks that encourage and motivate you.

Commit to regularly drawing from your well by engaging with these sources of inspiration and strength. For example, schedule regular meetings with your mentor, set aside time each day for your chosen practices, and actively participate in your community.

Knowing Your Source

Understanding the deeper sources of your desires is key to authentic action. Reflect on the core of who you are and your ultimate desires.

Knowing your Source involves understanding the deeper sources of your desires and what drives you. It's about connecting with your true self and gaining clarity on your ultimate desires and motivations. This self-awareness ensures that your actions are authentic and aligned with your true essence.

To know your Source, reflect on your deepest desires, values, and motivations. Consider what truly drives you and what you are passionate about. This might involve exploring your past experiences, identifying recurring themes in your life, and recognizing the qualities that define your true self.

Understanding your Source helps you make decisions that are in alignment with your authentic self. It ensures that your actions are driven by genuine desires rather than external pressures or societal expectations. By staying true to your core, you create a meaningful and fulfilling life.

Task: Reflect on the core of who you are and your ultimate desires. For instance, if you are driven by a desire to help others, consider the experiences that have shaped this motivation. If you are passionate about the environment, reflect on the activities that bring you joy and fulfillment in that area. If you are motivated by global issues, consider the qualities and values that define a journey that works toward making massive improvements.

Action Step: Journal about your core motivations and what drives your passion. For example:

- **Helping others:** Reflect on the experiences that have inspired your desire to help others and how this shapes your actions.

- **Social issues:** Consider the activities that bring you joy and fulfillment, and how they align with your true essence.

- **Global awareness:** Think about the qualities and values that define your journey and how they influence your decisions.

Use this reflection to ensure that your actions are aligned with your true self. Commit to making decisions and taking actions that resonate with your core motivations and ultimate desires.

Taking Inspired Actions

Inspired action is crucial for achieving your goals. Take one inspired action toward your vision today.

Taking inspired actions involves acting on the ideas and insights that resonate deeply with your passions and goals. Inspired actions are often driven by intuition and a sense of purpose. They feel aligned with your true self and are infused with enthusiasm and energy.

Inspired actions differ from routine or obligatory tasks because they come from a place of genuine motivation and excitement. These actions often lead to significant progress and breakthroughs, as they are fueled by a deep sense of alignment and purpose. When you take inspired actions, you move towards your goals with greater ease and joy.

To identify inspired actions, pay attention to the ideas and impulses that excite you. Consider the actions that feel most entrenched with your vision and purpose. Trust your intuition and allow yourself to be guided by your inner wisdom. Inspired actions often come with a sense of clarity and certainty, making them easier to execute.

Task: Take one inspired action toward your grand vision today. This could involve making a bold move, such as starting a new project or reaching out to a potential collaborator. For instance, if you have an idea for a new project that excites you, take the first step towards making it a reality. This might involve researching the feasibility of the project, creating a plan, or reaching out to potential partners. If there is someone you admire and would like to collaborate with, take the initiative to contact them and propose a collaboration.

Action Step: Identify an inspired action that aligns with your vision and take action immediately. For example:

- **Starting a new project:** Outline the steps needed to launch your project and take the first step, whether it's researching, planning, or reaching out to collaborators.

- **Reaching out to a collaborator:** Contact someone you admire and propose a collaboration, explaining how you can work together to achieve mutual goals.

- **Drawing out your vision with the right side of the brain**: Use creative techniques such as mind mapping, sketching, or visual brainstorming to explore and articulate your ideas. This approach engages the creative and intuitive aspects of your mind, helping you to see your vision from a new perspective.

Commit to taking inspired actions on a regular basis and notice how each step propels you toward your goals with greater ease and excitement. Taking action gets easier over time and with concerted effort and practice. Remember, the amount you put in directly reflects the amount you yield, so be sure to measure your results based on your input.

If you want more support or to surround yourself with ways to stay on task and experience greater results, I invite you to join *Ignite Your Billionaire Brand,* a weekly training that helps you create your deliverables. This program is designed to provide you with the tools, guidance, and community needed to effectively build and enhance your brand.

Ignite Your Billionaire Brand is not about accumulating wealth in dollars and cents; it's about creating a brand with a billion touchpoints and a billion impact markers. The true essence of a billionaire brand lies in its ability to reach and positively influence a billion people. This approach emphasizes working toward 'benevolent success,' where the primary goal is to make a substantial, meaningful difference in the lives of others rather than simply adding zeros to a bank account.

In building a billionaire brand, the focus is on impact, not income. Each session of *Ignite Your Billionaire Brand* is structured to help you refine your message, expand your reach, and amplify your impact. Whether through innovative marketing strategies, powerful touchpoints, or effective networking, this program equips you with the skills necessary to touch more lives and create lasting change.

By joining this community, you become part of a movement dedicated to achieving a new kind of success. You will connect with like-minded individuals who are also committed to making a difference. Together, you will share insights, support each other's growth, and celebrate each milestone on your journey to creating a billion touchpoints of positive impact. *Ignite Your Billionaire Brand* supports you every step of the way to build a legacy. You can join the program right now by using this *link* and start creating your billion touchpoints today.

Chapter 16

The Power of Giving First

The power of giving lies in its ability to transform both the giver and the recipient. *Giving* is not merely an act of charity but a profound expression of our humanity and connection to others. When we give, we extend a part of ourselves, whether it be our time, resources, or compassion, to uplift and support those around us. This act of selflessness creates a trust connection, spreading camaraderie and fostering a sense of community and interconnectedness. At its core, giving is about recognizing our shared humanity and taking steps to make the world a better place for everyone.

Engaging in acts of *giving* has a significant impact on personal growth and fulfillment. When we give, we step outside of our own concerns and focus on the needs and well-being of others. This shift in perspective cultivates empathy, compassion, and gratitude. It encourages us to develop a deeper understanding of the challenges faced by others and to appreciate the blessings in our own lives. Additionally, giving can lead to a sense of purpose and meaning as we see the positive impact of our actions and realize our potential to make a difference.

Giving strengthens the fabric of our communities. It fosters trust, cooperation, and a sense of shared responsibility. When individuals come together to support a common cause, they build bonds that transcend personal differences and create a united front against adversity. Whether it's through volunteering, donating, or simply offering a helping hand, acts of giving bring people closer together and create a more resilient and supportive community. This collective effort amplifies the impact of individual contributions, leading to meaningful and lasting change.

To maximize the impact of our giving, it's important to align our actions with our values and passions. When we give to causes that resonate with us, our contributions are more meaningful and fulfilling. This alignment ensures that our efforts are authentic and driven by genuine concern and commitment. By focusing on areas where we can make the most significant impact, we not only enhance the effectiveness of our giving but also reinforce our sense of purpose and connection to our legacy.

Giving

Days 21-30

Chapter 17

The Essence of Giving

The power of *giving* lies in its ability to transform both the giver and the recipient. Giving is not merely an act of charity; it is a profound expression of our humanity and our connection to others. When we give, we extend a part of ourselves, whether it be our time, resources, or compassion, to uplift and support those around us. At its core, *giving* is about recognizing our shared humanity and taking steps to make the world a better place for everyone.

Engaging in acts of *giving* has a significant impact on personal growth and fulfillment. When we give, we step outside of our own concerns and focus on the needs and well-being of others. This shift in perspective cultivates empathy, compassion, and gratitude. It encourages us to develop a deeper understanding of the challenges faced by others and to appreciate the blessings in our own lives. Additionally, *giving* can lead to a sense of purpose and meaning as we see the positive impact of our actions and realize our potential to make a difference.

Giving strengthens the fabric of our communities. It fosters trust, cooperation, and a sense of shared responsibility. When individuals come together to support a common cause, they build bonds that transcend personal differences and create a united front against adversity. This collective effort amplifies the impact of individual contributions, leading to meaningful and lasting change.

When we give to causes that resonate with us, our contributions are more meaningful and fulfilling. This alignment ensures that our efforts are authentic and driven by genuine concern and commitment. By focusing on areas where we can make the most significant impact, we not only enhance the effectiveness of our giving but also reinforce our sense of purpose and connection to our legacy.

Over the next 9 days, have fun *giving all you can*, not crumbs and tidbits, but all you have in spirit and effort.

The Power of Giving to Get

Giving leads to receiving and overall success. Plan a significant act of giving today.

The principle of *giving* to get is rooted in the idea that generosity creates a positive flow of energy that benefits both the giver and the receiver. When you give selflessly, you open up to receiving more in return. This principle is often referred to as the law of reciprocity, which states that acts of generosity create a ripple effect of positive energy and goodwill.

Giving can take many forms, from sharing your time and expertise to donating resources or offering support. It's about being generous with your resources and acting from a place of abundance. *Giving* selflessly creates a sense of connection and community, fostering a culture of kindness and cooperation.

The act of *giving* not only benefits others, but also enriches your own life. It creates a sense of fulfillment and purpose, enhances your well-being, and strengthens your relationships. By making *giving* a regular practice, you cultivate a positive mindset and attract more opportunities for growth and success.

Task: Plan a significant act of *giving* today. This could involve donating time, money, or resources to a cause you care about. For instance, you might donate to a local charity, volunteer your time at a community center, or offer your expertise to help someone in need. You could also support a friend or colleague by offering assistance with a project or providing mentorship and guidance.

Action Step: Choose a significant act of giving and take action today. For example:

- **Donate to a Local Charity:** Identify a charity that aligns with your values and make a donation.

- **Volunteer Your Time:** Find a volunteer opportunity that interests you and sign up to help.

- **Offer Your Expertise:** Reach out to someone who could benefit from your skills and offer your assistance.

Commit to giving as a regular practice, and notice how it enriches your life and the lives of others.

Defining Your Purpose

Staying true to your purpose is essential in your endeavors. Define your purpose and align it with your actions.

Defining your purpose involves understanding the deeper reasons behind your goals and actions. It's about connecting with what truly matters to you and aligning your efforts with a meaningful mission. When you have a clear sense of purpose, you are more motivated, focused, and resilient in the pursuit of your goals.

Your purpose serves as a guiding light, helping you navigate challenges and stay committed to your vision. It provides a sense of direction and clarity, ensuring that your actions are aligned with your long-term objectives. Defining your purpose also helps you prioritize your efforts and make decisions that support your mission.

To define your purpose, reflect on your values, passions, and the impact you want to make. Consider what drives you and what you want to achieve. Your purpose should resonate with your inner self and provide a strong foundation for your actions.

Task: Write a purpose statement that guides your decisions and actions. For instance, if you are passionate about education, your purpose statement might be: "To empower individuals through education and create opportunities for lifelong learning." If you are dedicated to improving health and wellness, your purpose statement might be: "To promote health and well-being through innovative solutions and compassionate care." If you aspire to make a positive impact in your community, your purpose statement might be: "To inspire positive change and contribute to the betterment of my community."

Action Step: Reflect on your values, passions, and the impact you want to make, and write a purpose statement that encapsulates your mission. For example:

- "To empower individuals through education and create opportunities for lifelong learning."
- "To promote health and well-being through innovative solutions and compassionate care."
- "To inspire positive change and contribute to the betterment of my community."

Align your actions with your purpose statement and regularly revisit it to ensure you stay true to your mission.

Focusing on Impact Over Individual Gain

Prioritizing impact over personal gain leads to more meaningful and lasting success. Identify how your actions can create a broader impact.

Focusing on impact over individual gain involves prioritizing actions that benefit others and contribute to the greater good. It's about shifting your perspective from self-interest to collective well-being. When you prioritize impact, you create more meaningful and lasting success, as your efforts are aligned with a higher purpose.

Impact-driven actions often have a ripple effect, creating positive outcomes that extend beyond your immediate circle. These actions contribute to the well-being of others and foster a sense of community and connection. By focusing on impact, you build a legacy that extends beyond personal achievements and benefits future generations.

To focus on impact, consider how your actions can create broader positive outcomes. Reflect on the ways you can contribute to your community, industry, or the world at large. Identify opportunities to make a difference and align your efforts with your desire to create positive change.

Task: Identify how your actions can create a broader impact. For instance, if you are an entrepreneur, consider how your products or services can address a widespread need and improve the lives of your customers. If you are a teacher or trainer, think about how your work can inspire and empower your students or clients. If you are involved in a community project, consider how your contributions can enhance the well-being of your community.

Action Step: Develop a plan to contribute to your community or industry in a meaningful way. For example:

- **As an Entrepreneur:** Create a product or service that addresses a widespread need and provides real value to your customers.

- **As a Teacher or Trainer:** Develop a program or course that inspires and empowers your students or clients.

- **As a Community Member:** Get involved in a community project that enhances the well-being of your neighborhood or city.

Commit to prioritizing impact over individual gain and regularly assess how your actions contribute to the greater good.

The Ripple Effect

One action can have far-reaching effects. Identify and plan an action with potential ripple effects.

The ripple effect refers to the idea that one action can create a series of positive outcomes that extend beyond the initial impact. It's about understanding how your actions can influence others and create a chain reaction of positive change. By recognizing the potential ripple effects of your actions, you can make more intentional and impactful choices.

To create a ripple effect, consider how your actions can inspire and benefit others. Reflect on the ways your efforts can create positive outcomes that extend beyond your immediate goals. Identify opportunities to make a difference and plan actions that have the potential to create a ripple effect of positive change.

The ripple effect highlights the interconnectedness of our actions and their impact on the world. When you take actions that create positive outcomes, you contribute to a broader culture of kindness, generosity, and growth. These actions inspire others to do the same, creating a multiplying effect that benefits many.

Task: Identify and plan an action with potential ripple effects. For instance, you might start a community project that addresses a local need and inspires others to get involved. This could involve organizing a neighborhood cleanup, starting a community garden, or launching a mentorship program. Another example might be mentoring someone in your field, providing guidance and support that helps them achieve their goals and inspires them to mentor others in the future.

Action Step: Choose an action that has the potential to create a ripple effect and take the first step today. For example:

- **Community Project:** Identify a local need and organize a project that addresses it. Reach out to neighbors or community members to get involved and collaborate on the initiative.

- **Mentorship:** Identify someone who could benefit from your guidance and offer to mentor them. Provide support, share your knowledge, and encourage them to pay it forward by mentoring others.

Commit to creating a ripple effect through your actions and regularly seek opportunities to make a positive difference.

Legacy is About Others

Shifting focus from self to others is key to creating a legacy. Plan an action that benefits others significantly.

Creating a lasting legacy involves shifting your focus from self-interest to the well-being of others. It's about understanding that true legacy is built through actions that benefit and uplift those around you. By prioritizing the needs and interests of others, you create a meaningful and enduring impact.

To create a legacy, consider how your actions can make a significant difference in the lives of others. Reflect on the ways you can contribute to the well-being and success of your family, friends, colleagues, and community. Identify opportunities to support, inspire, and empower others, and take intentional actions that create lasting positive change.

Legacy is about creating an imprint on the world that extends beyond your lifetime. It's about leaving a positive mark that continues to benefit others long after you are gone. By focusing on the needs of others, you build a legacy of kindness, generosity, and positive influence.

Task: Plan an action that benefits others significantly. For instance, you might create a scholarship fund to support students in need, start a volunteer group to address a community issue, or establish a mentorship program to help individuals achieve their goals. Another example might be creating a platform or initiative that empowers others to share their stories and experiences, fostering a sense of community and connection.

Action Step: Choose an action that has the potential to create a lasting positive impact and take the first step today. For example:

- **Scholarship Fund:** Identify a need for educational support and create a scholarship fund. Reach out to potential donors and set up a system for selecting and supporting recipients.

- **Volunteer Group:** Identify a community issue and organize a volunteer group to address it. Recruit volunteers, plan activities, and coordinate efforts to make a meaningful difference.

- **Mentorship Program:** Develop a mentorship program that connects mentors with individuals seeking guidance and support. Create a framework for the program, recruit mentors, and match them with mentees.

Commit to creating a legacy through your actions and regularly seek opportunities to make a significant difference in the lives of others.

Leaving an Imprint

Leaving a positive imprint on others is a vital aspect of legacy. Reflect on how you want to influence others positively.

Leaving an imprint involves creating a lasting positive influence on the lives of others. It's about understanding the impact of your actions and how they shape the experiences and perceptions of those around you. By leaving a positive imprint, you contribute to the well-being and growth of others, building a legacy of kindness and generosity.

To leave an imprint, consider how you want to be remembered and the qualities you want to be associated with your name. Reflect on the ways you can positively influence others through your actions, words, and presence. Identify opportunities to support, inspire, and uplift those around you, and make intentional choices that create a lasting positive impact.

Your imprint is created through the small, everyday actions that define your interactions with others. These actions, though seemingly insignificant, can have a profound and lasting effect on the lives of those you touch. By consistently acting with kindness, empathy, and integrity, you build a legacy of positive influence.

Task: Reflect on how you want to positively influence others and write letters of appreciation to people who have impacted your life. For instance, you might write a letter to a mentor who has guided you, a friend who has supported you, or a family member who has inspired you. Express your gratitude and share how their influence has shaped your life.

Action Step: Write letters of appreciation to individuals who have positively impacted your life. For example:

- **Mentor:** Write a letter to a mentor who has provided guidance and support. Share specific examples of how their mentorship has influenced your growth and success.

- **Friend:** Write a letter to a friend who has been there for you during challenging times. Express your gratitude for their support and friendship.

- **Family Member:** Write a letter to a family member who has inspired you. Reflect on the qualities and actions that have made a lasting impression on you.

Commit to regularly expressing appreciation and acknowledging the positive influence of others in your life. This practice not only strengthens your relationships, but also encourages others to continue making a positive impact.

Making a Billion Dollars by Impacting a Billion People

Substantial success requires a significant impact. Plan a strategy to impact a large number of people.

Making a billion dollars by impacting a billion people highlights the idea that substantial success is achieved through significant positive impact. It's about understanding that financial success and meaningful impact are interconnected. By focusing on creating value for a large number of people, you can achieve both financial prosperity and a lasting legacy.

To impact a billion people, consider how your products, services, or initiatives can address widespread needs and provide real value. Reflect on the ways you can leverage your skills, expertise, and resources to create solutions that benefit a large audience. Identify opportunities to scale your efforts and reach a broader audience, ensuring that your impact extends far and wide.

Creating a significant impact requires a clear vision, strategic planning, and a commitment to continuous improvement. By aligning your efforts with a higher purpose and focusing on creating value for others, you can achieve substantial success and build a legacy of positive influence.

Task: Plan a strategy to impact a large number of people. For instance, you might develop a product or service that addresses a widespread need, such as a health and wellness app that provides accessible and affordable resources for improving physical and mental well-being. Alternatively, you might create an online platform that connects individuals with opportunities for education and personal development, making valuable resources available to a global audience.

Action Step: Develop a plan to create a significant impact and reach a large audience. For example:

- Product or Service: Identify a widespread need and develop a product or service that addresses it. Research your target audience, create a detailed plan, and take the first steps toward bringing your idea to life.

- Online Platform: Create an online platform that connects individuals with valuable resources and opportunities. Develop a clear vision, outline the features and benefits of the platform, and start building and promoting it.

Commit to continuously refining and scaling your efforts to maximize your impact and reach a broader audience.

Giving for the Good of Others

Understanding the true essence of giving is crucial. Commit to a long-term giving initiative.

Giving for the good of others involves understanding the true essence of generosity and its impact on both the giver and the receiver. It's about recognizing that acts of giving create a positive flow of energy and contribute to the well-being of individuals and communities. By committing to a long-term giving initiative, you make a sustained positive impact and build a legacy of compassion and generosity.

The essence of giving lies in selflessness and a genuine desire to help others. It's about being generous with your time, resources, and support, without expecting anything in return. When you give selflessly, you create a sense of connection and community, fostering a culture of kindness and cooperation.

A long-term giving initiative involves committing to a cause or project that aligns with your values and passions. It requires dedication, planning, and ongoing effort to ensure that your contributions make a meaningful and lasting impact. By focusing on long-term giving, you create a sustained positive influence that extends beyond immediate acts of generosity.

Task: Commit to a long-term giving initiative, such as partnering with a nonprofit organization for ongoing support. For instance, you might partner with an organization that provides educational resources to underserved communities, offering financial support, volunteer time, or expertise. Alternatively, you might commit to supporting environmental conservation efforts by donating to organizations that protect natural habitats and promote sustainability.

Action Step: Choose a long-term giving initiative that aligns with your values and passions, and take the first steps to get involved. For example:

- **Partner With a Nonprofit:** Identify a nonprofit organization that aligns with your values and reaches out to explore partnership opportunities. Offer financial support, volunteer time, or expertise to help advance their mission.

- **Support Environmental Conservation:** Research organizations that focus on environmental conservation and commit to supporting their efforts. Make regular donations, participate in volunteer activities, and advocate for sustainability initiatives.

Commit to making long-term giving a regular practice and regularly assess the impact of your contributions to ensure they are making a meaningful difference.

Thinking Beyond Oneself

Legacy requires a broader view of the world. Expand your vision to include global impact.

Thinking beyond oneself involves expanding your perspective to consider the broader impact of your actions on the world. It's about understanding that legacy is not just about personal achievements but also about contributing to the well-being and growth of humanity. By adopting a global perspective, you ensure that your efforts create positive change on a larger scale.

To think beyond oneself, reflect on the interconnectedness of your actions and their impact on the world. Consider how your efforts can address global challenges and contribute to the betterment of society. Identify opportunities to make a difference on a larger scale and align your actions with a higher purpose.

Expanding your vision to include global impact requires a commitment to continuous learning and growth. Stay informed about global issues and trends, and seek out opportunities to contribute to solutions. By thinking beyond oneself, you create a legacy that extends beyond personal achievements and benefits future generations.

Task: Expand your vision to include global impact and identify ways to contribute to global challenges. For instance, you might focus on addressing issues such as poverty, education, health, or environmental sustainability. Consider how your skills, expertise, and resources can make a difference on a larger scale. For example, if you are passionate about education, you might support initiatives that provide access to quality education for underserved communities worldwide. If you are dedicated to health and wellness, you might contribute to efforts that improve healthcare access and outcomes in developing countries.

Action Step: Identify a global issue that resonates with you and take action to contribute to a solution. For example:

- **Education:** Support initiatives that provide access to quality education for underserved communities worldwide. This could involve donating to organizations that build schools, provide educational resources, or offer scholarships to students in need.

- **Health:** Contribute to efforts that improve healthcare access and outcomes in developing countries. This could involve supporting organizations that provide medical supplies, train healthcare workers, or offer preventive health programs.

Commit to regularly expanding your vision and seeking opportunities to make a positive global impact. Stay informed about global issues and trends, and continuously look for ways to contribute to solutions.

The Longevity of Humanity and Goodness in Society

Ensuring your legacy contributes to the long-term good of humanity is paramount. Plan a sustainable action that benefits society.

Ensuring your legacy contributes to the long-term good of humanity involves focusing on actions that have a lasting positive impact on society. It's about understanding that legacy is not just about immediate achievements but also about creating sustainable change that benefits future generations. By planning sustainable actions, you ensure that your efforts contribute to the well-being and growth of humanity.

Sustainability involves considering the long-term effects of your actions and making choices that promote enduring positive outcomes. It's about being mindful of the resources you use and the impact you have on the environment, society, and future generations. Sustainable actions create a legacy of responsibility, stewardship, and positive influence.

To plan a sustainable action, reflect on the ways your efforts can create lasting positive change. Identify opportunities to support initiatives that promote sustainability and address long-term challenges. Consider how your skills, resources, and expertise can contribute to solutions that benefit society as a whole.

Task: Plan a sustainable action that benefits society, such as supporting environmental conservation efforts, promoting social justice, or advancing sustainable development goals. For instance, you might commit to reducing your carbon footprint by adopting eco-friendly practices, supporting organizations that protect natural habitats, or advocating for policies that promote environmental sustainability. Alternatively, you might focus on promoting social justice by supporting initiatives that address inequality, discrimination, and human rights.

Action Step: Choose a sustainable action that aligns with your values and take the first steps to implement it. For example:

- **Environmental Conservation:** Commit to reducing your carbon footprint by adopting eco-friendly practices, such as using renewable energy, reducing waste, and supporting sustainable products. Get involved in efforts to protect natural habitats and advocate for environmental policies.

- **Social Justice:** Support initiatives that promote social justice and address inequality, discrimination, and human rights. This could involve donating to organizations that advocate for marginalized communities, volunteering your time to support social justice causes, or raising awareness about important issues.

Commit to making sustainability a core principle in your efforts and regularly assess the impact of your actions to ensure they are contributing to the long-term good of humanity.

Chapter 18

Let's Celebrate

Congratulations on finishing a life-changing *30 Ways to Ignite Your Legacy in 30 days*. Bravo and well done on completing the steps, learning the pillars, and uncovering new ideas around your desired legacy. This is just the beginning of a wonderful relationship with you and your legacy. I hope that the 30 steps awakened some ideas and percolated to the surface a bigger vision for your legacy. Each step is just a starting point of what you can achieve and where you can expand upon your lasting legacy.

Remember that your legacy is shaped by the choices you make and the actions you take every day. Stay true to your core values and mission, and let them guide your efforts. Embrace the principles of the IGNITE frequency—Inspire, Give, Nurture, Improve, Transform, Empower—and integrate them into your daily life. And, hold the pillars of KNOWING, DOING, and GIVING close to your heart.

As you continue your journey, remain open to new opportunities for growth and impact. Seek out ways to expand your vision and contribute to the well-being of humanity. Stay committed to your purpose and take inspired actions that align with your goals. By doing so, you create a legacy that reflects your true essence and makes a meaningful difference in the world.

You have the power to *Ignite Your Legacy* and create a lasting positive impact. Every small action you take contributes to the greater good and shapes the world around you. Stay focused on your mission, embrace the principles of the IGNITE frequency, and continue to take inspired actions that align with your purpose.

Legacy Intentions

Remember that legacy is not just about personal achievements but about contributing to the well-being and growth of humanity. By giving selflessly, thinking beyond yourself, and prioritizing impact, you create a legacy of kindness, generosity, and positive influence.

Your journey to igniting your legacy is a testament to your dedication, passion, and commitment to making a difference. Keep moving forward with confidence and determination, knowing that your efforts are creating a better future for yourself and others.

Thank you for embarking on this transformative journey to ignite your legacy. Your actions carry immense weight, and the benefits of your influence will be felt for generations to come. Keep shining your light and continue to inspire others to do the same. Together, we can cultivate a world overflowing with goodness, compassion, and positive change.

In sharing these ideas with you and encouraging you to build your legacy, I too am nurturing my own. If something I have said here propels you forward on your path, then your legacy will change lives, and my small contribution to your journey will become a cherished part of my own legacy.

Legacy Success

As you grow in your legacy endeavors, you may one day reach a point where you can mentor and guide someone else. Imagine the joy of watching another soul blossom under your tutelage, their own legacy intertwining with yours. Each time we help another and become an integral cog in the collective, we elevate the consciousness, uplift the human spirit, amplify the realm of possibility, and make the world a more endearing place for all to thrive and prosper.

Your legacy is not just a personal pursuit—it is a gift to humanity. Keep moving forward, my friend, for your actions have the power to transform lives, communities, and the very fabric of our shared existence. The world is waiting to witness the profound impact of your life's work.

Bonus

Chapter 19

Bonus Content to Grow Your Legacy

*I*t's easy to feel overwhelmed by the magnitude of the challenges we face in today's world—poverty, inequality, climate change, and so much more. But when we focus on the power of legacy, we realize that each of us has the ability to make a meaningful impact, no matter how small it may seem. As you continue to build your legacy, you begin to see the rewarding effects of your actions spreading out into the world. Your small acts of kindness, words of encouragement, and commitment to making a difference all contribute to a larger wave of positive change.

Bonus 1

Ignite Your Breakthrough

*E*mbarking on the journey to build a legacy begins with a transformative breakthrough. This initial step is crucial, as it involves breaking free from the limitations and barriers that have held you back. Without overcoming these obstacles, it's challenging to reach your full potential and make a significant impact. *Ignite Your Breakthrough* is designed to help you identify these barriers, develop strategies to overcome them, and set a strong foundation for your legacy journey.

In working on your breakthrough, you will delve into the process of identifying personal and professional obstacles that may be hindering your progress. These could range from self-doubt and fear of failure to external challenges such as lack of resources or support. Understanding these obstacles is the first step toward addressing them effectively.

Breakthrough work means exploring practical strategies to facilitate mindset shifts, resilience-building techniques, and the invaluable benefits of overcoming limiting beliefs. By taking the time to facilitate a breakthrough, you overcome the setbacks and reframe your thinking to support solutions and possibilities where there once was none. Breakthrough awakens the mind to what is possible and what the mind can *perceive it can achieve.*

Identifying Your Obstacles

- **Reflect on Past Experiences**: Look back at past experiences to uncover patterns or events that may have contributed to current challenges. Journaling and introspection can be effective tools in this process.

- **Self-Assessment Tools**: Utilize self-assessment tools and frameworks to identify specific areas for improvement. Personality tests, SWOT analysis, and feedback from peers can provide valuable insights.

- **Set clear goals**: Establishing clear, actionable goals can help you focus on overcoming specific obstacles. Break down these goals into manageable steps to track your progress.

Strategies for Breakthroughs

- **Embrace a growth mindset**: Adopting a growth mindset involves believing in your ability to learn and grow. This mindset shift can empower you to tackle challenges with confidence.

- **Develop resilience**: Building resilience involves learning to adapt and bounce back from setbacks. Techniques such as mindfulness, stress management, and positive thinking can enhance your resilience.

- **Seek feedback and mentorship**: Constructive feedback and guidance from mentors can accelerate your progress. Mentors provide valuable perspectives and support that can help you navigate challenges.

Benefits of Breaking Through

- **Clarity and focus**: Achieving a breakthrough provides clarity on your goals and the steps needed to achieve them. This focus can lead to more effective decision-making and strategic planning.

- **New opportunities**: Overcoming obstacles can open up new opportunities for personal and professional growth. You may discover new skills, passions, or career paths.

- **Personal fulfillment**: The sense of accomplishment from achieving a breakthrough can lead to increased confidence and fulfillment. This positive momentum can propel you towards your legacy goals.

The Power of Mentoring

- **Insights from experienced Mentors**: Mentors offer insights based on their own experiences and expertise. This guidance can help you avoid common pitfalls and make informed decisions.

- **Personalized guidance**: Mentors provide personalized advice and support tailored to your specific needs and goals. This individualized approach can enhance your growth and development.

- **Community and accountability**: Being part of a mentoring community fosters a sense of belonging and accountability. Sharing your journey with others can motivate you to stay committed to your goals.

Join the Ignite Your Breakthrough Program

Ignite Your Breakthrough is a transformative mastermind focused on building your mental mindset for your legacy. By identifying and overcoming obstacles, embracing a growth mindset, and seeking mentorship, you can unlock your full potential and set a strong foundation for your legacy journey. With clarity, focus, and resilience, you are well-equipped to achieve your dreams and make a lasting impact. Classes take place each week, *sign up here or click to find out more*, otherwise email *support@igniteyou.life*, or book a discovery call at *calendly.com/jbtime*.

Bonus 2

Ignite Your Solo Book

Writing a solo book is a powerful and enduring way to share your knowledge, experiences, and vision with the world. It serves as a testament to your expertise and a tangible piece of your legacy. Through the *Ignite Your Solo Book* program, we will guide you through the entire process of conceptualizing, writing, publishing, and marketing your book. This journey not only solidifies your authority in your field but also amplifies your impact and reaches a broader audience.

In this weekly program, we will explore the reasons why writing a book is a crucial step in legacy building. We will provide a detailed roadmap to help you navigate each phase of the book-writing process, from choosing a compelling topic to finalizing the manuscript. Additionally, we will discuss effective strategies for publishing and marketing your book to ensure it reaches and resonates with your target audience.

Throughout this program, you will have a clear understanding of the steps involved in writing a book and the immense value it brings to your legacy. You will be equipped with the knowledge and tools to embark on your book-writing journey and create a lasting impact through your words.

Why Write a Book?

- **Establish authority**: Writing a book positions you as an expert in your field. It showcases your knowledge and insights, earning you credibility and respect.

- **Reach a wider audience**: A book allows you to reach a global audience, sharing your message far and wide. This increased visibility can open up new opportunities for collaboration and influence.

- **Create lasting impact**: Books have the power to inspire, educate, and transform lives. By sharing your story and insights, you can create a lasting impact on readers and contribute to their growth and development.

Steps to Writing Your Book

- **Choose a compelling topic**: Identify a topic that resonates with your audience and aligns with your expertise. Consider what unique insights or perspectives you can offer.

- **Outline your book's structure**: Create a detailed outline to organize your thoughts and ensure a logical flow. Break down your content into chapters and subtopics for easy navigation.

- **Write consistently**: Set aside dedicated time for writing and establish a routine. Consistency is key to making steady progress and completing your manuscript.

Publishing and Marketing

- **Explore publishing options**: Decide whether to pursue traditional publishing or self-publishing. Each option has its pros and cons, so choose the one that best fits your goals and resources.

- **Develop a marketing plan**: Create a comprehensive marketing plan to promote your book. Utilize social media, email marketing, and book launch events to generate buzz and attract readers.

- **Leverage online platforms**: Use online platforms such as Amazon, Goodreads, and your own website to reach a broader audience. Engage with readers through reviews, discussions, and promotions.

Benefits of Having a Solo Book

- **Enhance your brand**: A book enhances your personal and professional brand, showcasing your expertise and elevating your reputation.

- **Additional income streams**: Book sales can create additional income streams, and speaking engagements and workshops based on your book can further increase your earnings.

- **Leave a tangible legacy**: A book is a tangible piece of your legacy that can be passed down through generations. It serves as a lasting testament to your knowledge and contributions.

Join the Ignite Your Solo Book Program

Ignite Your Solo Book is a powerful way to share your legacy with the world. By connecting with other authors in this immersive program, you can create a compelling and impactful book that enhances your authority, reaches a wider audience, and leaves a lasting legacy. With the right guidance and support, you can bring your book to life and make a meaningful contribution to your field and the lives of your readers. Classes take place each week, *sign up here or click to find out more*, otherwise email *support@igniteyou.life*, or book a discovery call at *calendly.com/jbtime*.

Bonus 3

Ignite Your Signature Talk

Public speaking is one of the most effective ways to share your legacy with a broad audience. A well-crafted and delivered signature talk can captivate and inspire, leaving a lasting impression on your listeners. *Ignite Your Signature Talk* is designed to help you develop and deliver a powerful presentation that showcases your expertise and vision. This award-winning program will support you through the process of crafting your talk, perfecting your delivery, and promoting your message to reach a wider audience.

We will begin by discussing the importance of a signature talk and how it can elevate your legacy. You will learn how to identify your key message, structure your talk, and use storytelling techniques to engage your audience. Additionally, the program provides practical tips for delivering your talk with confidence and impact, including body language, vocal variety, and audience interaction.

Promoting your signature talk is equally important to ensure it reaches and resonates with your target audience. This enjoyable program offers strategies for leveraging online platforms, seeking speaking opportunities, and collaborating with organizations to maximize your visibility. By the end of this course, you will be equipped with the skills and knowledge to *Ignite Your Signature Talk* and make a lasting impact through public speaking.

Crafting Your Signature Talk

- **Identify your key message**: Determine the core message you want to convey to your audience. This message should align with your legacy goals and resonate with your listeners.

- **Structure your talk**: Organize your talk with a clear beginning, middle, and end. Start with a strong opening to capture attention, develop your key points in the middle, and end with a memorable conclusion.

- **Use storytelling techniques**: Incorporate storytelling to make your talk more engaging and relatable. Share personal anecdotes, case studies, and examples to illustrate your points and connect with your audience emotionally.

Delivering Your Talk

- **Practice your delivery**: Practice your talk multiple times to build confidence and refine your delivery. Pay attention to your pacing, tone, and articulation.

- **Use body language**: Use positive body language to enhance your message. Maintain eye contact, use gestures to emphasize points, and move around the stage to engage with your audience.

- **Engage with your audience**: Interact with your audience through questions, polls, and discussions. Encourage participation and make your talk a two-way conversation to keep your audience engaged.

Promoting Your Talk

- **Leverage online platforms**: Share your talk on online platforms such as YouTube™, LinkedIn™, and your website. Use social media to promote your talk and reach a wider audience.

- **Seek speaking opportunities**: Look for speaking opportunities at conferences, workshops, and events. Submit proposals to speak at industry events and join speaker bureaus to increase your visibility.

- **Collaborate with organizations**: Partner with organizations, companies, and media outlets to promote your talk. Collaboration can help you reach new audiences and enhance your credibility.

Benefits of a Signature Talk

- **Establish thought leadership**: A signature talk establishes you as a thought leader in your field. It showcases your expertise and provides a platform to share your vision.

- **Inspire and influence**: Your talk can inspire and influence others, spreading your message and values. This impact contributes to your legacy and helps you achieve your long-term goals.

- **Create new opportunities**: Delivering a successful talk can lead to new opportunities, such as speaking engagements, consulting work, and collaborations. These opportunities can further enhance your legacy.

Join *Ignite Your Signature Talk*

Ignite Your Signature Talk is a powerful way to share your legacy with the world. By crafting a compelling message, delivering it with confidence, and promoting it effectively, you can captivate and inspire your audience. With the right preparation and strategies, you can use public speaking to make a lasting impact and achieve your legacy goals. This program also has a certification and the ability to be part of the *Ignite Speaker Bureau*. Classes take place each week, *sign up here or click to find out more*, otherwise email *support@ igniteyou.life*, or book a discovery call at *calendly.com/jbtime*.

Bonus 4

Ignite Your Billionaire Brand

In the modern world, a strong personal brand is essential for building a legacy. Your brand is a reflection of your values, vision, and expertise, and it plays a crucial role in how you are perceived by others. *Ignite Your Billionaire Brand* is designed to help you create a powerful and recognizable brand that stands out in a crowded marketplace. This extensive brand-building program guides you through the process of defining, building, and maintaining your brand, ensuring it resonates with your audience and supports your legacy goals.

The program starts by exploring the importance of a strong brand and the key elements that define it. You will learn how to articulate your unique strengths and qualities, develop a clear brand message, and create a visual identity that captures your essence. Additionally, we will discuss strategies for building and promoting your brand through various channels, including social media, online platforms, and collaborations.

Maintaining your brand's integrity and relevance over time is equally important. Participating in this program will provide insights into monitoring your brand's performance, staying true to your values, and continuously innovating to stay ahead. As you learn more, you will have a comprehensive understanding of how to ignite your billionaire brand and leverage it to achieve your legacy goals.

Defining Your Brand

- **Identify your unique strengths**: Reflect on what makes you unique. Consider your skills, experiences, and passions, and how they differentiate you from others in your field.

- **Develop a clear brand message**: Craft a concise and compelling brand message that communicates your value proposition. This message should resonate with your target audience and reflect your core values.

- **Create a visual identity**: Design a visual identity that aligns with your brand message. This includes your logo, color scheme, typography, and overall aesthetic. Consistency in your visual identity helps create a memorable and recognizable brand.

Building Your Brand

- **Utilize social media**: Leverage social media platforms to establish your presence and engage with your audience. Share valuable content, interact with followers, and build a community around your brand.

- **Engage with your audience**: Foster meaningful connections with your audience through consistent interactions. Respond to comments, ask for feedback, and show appreciation for their support.

- **Collaborate with influencers**: Partner with influencers and industry leaders to expand your reach. Collaborations can introduce your brand to new audiences and enhance your credibility.

Maintaining Your Brand

- **Monitor performance**: Regularly assess your brand's performance using analytics and feedback. Identify areas for improvement and adjust your strategies accordingly.

- **Stay true to your values**: Ensure that your actions and communications consistently reflect your brand values. Authenticity is key to building trust and loyalty with your audience.

- **Innovate and evolve**: Continuously seek opportunities to innovate and evolve your brand. Stay informed about industry trends and be willing to adapt to changes to remain relevant.

Benefits of a Strong Brand

- **Recognition and credibility**: A strong brand enhances your recognition and credibility, making it easier to attract opportunities and partnerships.

- **Attract opportunities**: A well-established brand can attract various opportunities, including speaking engagements, collaborations, and media coverage.

- **Inspire and influence**: Your brand can inspire and influence others, spreading your values and vision far and wide. This impact contributes to your legacy and helps you achieve your long-term goals.

Join Ignite Your Billionaire Brand

Igniting Your Billionaire Brand is a vital component of building your legacy. By defining, building, and maintaining a strong personal brand, you can create a lasting impact and achieve your legacy goals. With a clear brand message, consistent engagement, and continuous innovation, you can establish a powerful and recognizable brand that resonates with your audience and supports your journey toward legacy building. Classes take place each week, *sign up here or to find out more*, otherwise email *support@igniteyou.life*, or book a discovery call at *calendly.com/jbtime*.

Bonus 5

The Power of the Ignite Your Legacy Program

The *Ignite Your Legacy* Mentoring Program stands out because it integrates four powerful programs into one comprehensive approach to legacy building. By focusing on breakthroughs, book writing, branding, and public speaking, this program provides a holistic and strategic path to creating a lasting impact. It includes the unique benefits of each of the four Ignite programs and illustrates how they collectively contribute to building a legacy.

Building a legacy requires a multifaceted approach that encompasses personal growth, knowledge sharing, brand development, and effective communication. Each program within the *Ignite Your Legacy* mentoring program addresses a crucial aspect of legacy building, ensuring you have the tools and support needed to achieve your goals. From overcoming obstacles to establishing your authority and sharing your vision with the world, these programs provide a comprehensive framework for success.

Additionally, the entire program utilizes the invaluable role of mentoring, the benefits of working within a group, and the unique advantages of partnering with Lady JB Owen. Her expertise and experience as an award-winning humanitarian, speaker, mentor, trainer, and philanthropist make her the ideal guide for your legacy journey. By the end of this summary, you will understand how the *Ignite Your Legacy* Mentoring Program can empower you to build a meaningful and lasting legacy.

Benefits of the Program

- **Comprehensive guidance**: The program offers comprehensive guidance in key areas of legacy building, including breakthroughs, book writing, branding, and public speaking. This holistic approach ensures you are well-prepared to achieve your legacy goals.

- **Personalized mentoring**: With personalized mentoring from Lady JB Owen, you receive tailored advice and support to navigate your unique challenges and opportunities. Her expertise and insights can accelerate your progress and enhance your results.

- **Community and accountability**: Joining a community of like-minded individuals provides a supportive environment for growth. The accountability and encouragement from peers can motivate you to stay committed and achieve your goals.

The Role of Mentoring

- **Expert advice and insights**: Mentors offer expert advice and insights based on their own experiences and knowledge. This guidance can help you make informed decisions and avoid common pitfalls.

- **Continuous motivation**: Mentors provide continuous motivation and support, helping you stay focused and driven. Their encouragement can boost your confidence and keep you on track towards your goals.

- **Supportive community**: Being part of a mentoring community fosters a sense of belonging and camaraderie. Sharing your journey with others creates a collaborative environment for growth and success.

Why Choose Lady JB Owen?

- **Award-winning Humanitarian**: Lady JB Owen is an award-winning humanitarian with a proven track record of making a positive impact. Her dedication to philanthropy and community service reflects her commitment to building a legacy.

- **Experienced Speaker and Mentor**: With extensive experience as a speaker and mentor, Lady JB Owen brings valuable expertise to the program. Her insights and guidance can help you achieve your legacy goals.

- **Philanthropist and Trainer**: Lady JB Owen's background as a philanthropist and trainer adds depth to her mentoring approach. Her comprehensive knowledge and skills make her the perfect guide for your legacy journey.

Join Ignite Your Legacy

Building a legacy requires a multifaceted approach that considers your business, brand, book, and public speaking skills. *The Ignite Your Legacy* mentoring program provides the tools, support, and guidance needed to achieve your ultimate legacy goals. Working with Lady JB Owen and leveraging her expertise will empower you to create products and services that support your legacy and make a lasting impact. By integrating breakthroughs, book writing, branding, and public speaking, this program offers a holistic path to legacy building, ensuring you are well-equipped to leave a meaningful and enduring legacy.

To truly I*gnite Your Legacy*, you must be willing to take bold action and step outside your comfort zone. This means working on your personal development, enhancing your skills, building your business, and shaping your unique philosophies with the world.

As we conclude *30 Ways to Ignite Your Legacy in 30 Days*, remember that each day offers a new opportunity to make a lasting impact. Your legacy is built through the choices you make, the kindness you extend, and the passion you pursue. Embrace the journey with courage and conviction, knowing that your efforts today will inspire future generations.

Over the past 30 days, you have explored ways to break through obstacles, share your wisdom through writing, build a powerful brand, and deliver compelling messages. Each of these steps is a building block in creating a legacy that will endure. The path may not always be easy, but it is in these moments of challenge that your true character and resilience shine through.

Your legacy is not just a reflection of your achievements, but of the lives you touch and the positive change you bring about. By living intentionally and with purpose, you set an example for others to follow. Every small act of kindness, every bold decision, and every effort to make a difference contributes to a greater whole.

As you move forward, remember that your legacy is a living, evolving testament to who you are and what you stand for. Continue to dream big, act boldly, and lead with your heart. Surround yourself with those who inspire you, challenge you, and support you on this journey. Together, you can create a ripple effect of positive change that extends far beyond your immediate reach.

Let this book serve as both a guide and a source of inspiration as you continue to build your legacy. Your journey is just beginning, and the world is waiting for the unique impact only you can make. Go forth with confidence, knowing that you have the power to leave a lasting, meaningful legacy. Here's to your ongoing adventure and the extraordinary legacy you are destined to create.

Author Biography

Lady JB Owen is a fearless female leader, 25-time bestselling author, global publisher, international brand builder, award-winning businesswoman, celebrated humanitarian, coveted speaker, trainer, legacy mentor, and knight lady. JB's entrepreneurial spirit and dedication to making a positive impact have led her to combine business with inspiration in an innovative way. Forbes Magazine has dubbed JB the "Heart-Centered Publisher," Entrepreneur Magazine has called her a "Female Entrepreneur Determined to Change the World," and Apple News added her name to their "Top 50 Entrepreneurs to Watch." She combines purpose, passion, and possibilities in everything she does on her mission to Ignite every life on the planet and create a ripple effect of change.

As founder and CEO of Ignite Publishing™, the leader in Empowerment Publishing, Lady JB has published over 800 authors from 47 countries, going international best-sellers in 13 countries in 197 categories. Her goal is to inspire others through Ignite Moments™, those moments that inspired individuals to empower others. As a publisher, she teaches individuals how to tell their stories in a way that transforms their lives and empowers them to create the lives they envision for themselves and others. As a Legacy Mentor, she mentors on giving back, raising the consciousness, and creating lasting impact for future generations. Lady JB believes we all can ignite our lives, the lives of others, and humanity.

Lady JB is also the CEO of JBO Global™, which produces award-winning, eco-friendly products. She is an Executive Producer at Ignite Moments Media™ and is devoted to the betterment of others through the power of uplifting one another.

In recognition of her profound humanitarian and entrepreneurial efforts, Lady JB was knighted by the Royal Order of St. Constantine the Great and St. Helen in 2022. Her humanitarian work spans building a school in impoverished areas , spearheading the Ignite Humanity global movement, and establishing the Ignite Humanity Foundation Fund. In her relentless pursuit to raise awareness of literacy, she has cycled thousands of kilometers for charity, including a journey to Alaska, across Canada, and to Mexico with her husband on their tandem bike. Her humanitarian work was further honored in 2022 when she was bestowed with the Ignite Humanitarian Award at the *Be Great!* Foundation.

Lady JB Owen combines purpose, passion, and possibilities in everything she does on her mission to Ignite every life on the planet and create a ripple effect of change. She believes that when we come together in unity and harmony with the desire to raise the consciousness of all humanity, magic will happen.

She is the mother of two children and two stepchildren and lives in Canada with her husband, Peter. She travels extensively, has new adventures, and reminds everyone that *anything and everything is possible*.

Contact Lady JB Owen

http://calendly.com/jbtime
info@igniteyou.life

Websites:
www.jbowen.website

Socials:
FB: Lady JB Owen
IG: Lady JB Owen
LinkedIn: Lady JB Owen

Contact Ignite
support@igniteyou.life

Websites:
www.igniteyou.life
www.ignitehumanity.life

Programs:
courses.igniteinstitute.life/igniteyourlegacy
courses.igniteinstitute.life/breakthrough
courses.igniteinstitute.life/billionairebrand
courses.igniteinstitute.life/solobookclub
courses.igniteinstitute.life/innercircle
https://market.igniteyou.life/join-ignite-inspires

Socials:
FB: Ignite Humanity Community
          Ignite You
          Ignite Possibilities
          Ignite Moments

IG: Ignite You

Charity Initiatives:

ignitehumanity.life/donate

Free Ebook

https://forgiveness.igniteyou.life/ebook
https://market.igniteyou.life/writingprompts

Free Meditation

https://affirmations.thepinkbillionaire.com

Free TV Episodes

https://watch.ignitehumanity.life/

Book recommendations:

Awaken Giants by Tony Robbins

Think and Grow Rich by Napoleon Hill

E-Myth by Michael E. Gerber

The 10X Rule by Grant Cardone

The Greatest Salesman in the World by Og Mandino

The Science of Getting Rich by Wallace D. Wattles

Good to Great by James C. Collins

Big Magic by Elizabeth Gilbert

Intellectual Property

The 30 Ways to Ignite Your Legacy in 30 Days system is the intellectual property of Lady JB Owen. All rights reserved.

Insights

Ideas

Ideas

Plans

Plans

Dreams